As one of the world's longest established and best-known travel brands, Thomas Cook are the experts in travel.

For more than 135 years our guidebooks have unlocked the secrets of destinations around the world, sharing with travellers a wealth of experience and a passion for travel.

Rely on Thomas Cook as your travelling companion on your next trip and benefit from our unique heritage.

Thomas Cook **pocket** guides

REYKJAVIK

GW00514736

Thomas
Cook

Your travelling companion since 1873

Written by Ethel Davies
Updated by Eliza Reid

Published by Thomas Cook Publishing
A division of Thomas Cook Tour Operations Limited
Company registration No: 3772199 England
The Thomas Cook Business Park, 9 Coningsby Road
Peterborough PE3 8SB, United Kingdom
Email: books@thomascook.com, Tel: +44 (0)1733 416477
www.thomascookpublishing.com

Produced by The Content Works Ltd
Aston Court, Kingsmead Business Park, Frederick Place
High Wycombe, Bucks HP11 1LA
www.thecontentworks.com

Series design based on an original concept by Studio 183 Limited

ISBN: 978-1-84848-287-6

First edition © 2006 Thomas Cook Publishing
This third edition © 2010 Thomas Cook Publishing
Text © Thomas Cook Publishing
Maps © Thomas Cook Publishing/PCGraphics (UK) Limited
Transport map © Communicarta Limited

Series Editor: Lucy Armstrong
Production/DTP: Steven Collins

Printed and bound in Spain by GraphyCems

Cover photography (Viking helmet, Viking festival, Hafnarfjörður) © Hemis/Alamy

CONTENTS

SYMBOLS KEY

The following symbols are used throughout this book:

ⓐ address   ☎ telephone   ⓦ website address   ⓔ email
🕒 opening times   Ⓝ public transport connections

The following symbols are used on the maps:

🛈	information office	▦	points of interest
✈	airport	○	city
➕	hospital	○	large town
🛡	police station	○	small town
🚌	bus station	—	main road
✝	cathedral	—	minor road
❶	numbers denote featured cafés & restaurants		

Hotels and restaurants are graded by approximate price as follows:
£ budget price   ££ mid-range price   £££ expensive

◑ *Contrasting old and new church spires dominate the city's skyline*

INTRODUCING
Reykjavik

Introduction

It's hard to explain Reykjavik's allure. Architecturally, it is not a magnificent city, and even within the framework of Iceland, its weather can be rather grey. It is not particularly well planned: drab apartment blocks stretch out from the historic centre for many more kilometres than its population of 200,000 warrants, and the public transportation system is somewhat haphazard.

And yet Reykjavik draws visitors in year after year, many of whom leave with plans for their next trip in tow. After a few days or a week taking in the city's low horizon, its spectacular backdrop of mountains and sea, and its clutch of inviting shops, cafés and pubs, Iceland's intimate, plucky spirit starts to come into focus. Unlike many international cities, you will leave Reykjavik feeling you had a glimpse of the nation's soul.

With a strong Nordic heritage that can be traced back to individual Vikings from Norway, Icelandic words have barely changed from the language spoken by those first settlers, yet everyone also speaks English. The country is young, both physically, with active volcanoes still creating land, and administratively, with the establishment of independence from Denmark occurring in only 1944.

The global financial crisis in 2008 hit Iceland hard, causing all of its major banks to collapse and the government to fall, and forcing the nation to seek a loan from the International Monetary Fund. A new left-wing coalition government was elected in early 2009. The country still maintains a strong social safety net, however, and life expectancy is one of the highest in the world. Residents of Reykjavik generally live well, although previously decadent lifestyles have been somewhat curtailed due to high inflation, interest rates, and unemployment. Energy production and tourism, along with the traditionally strong fishing sector, are expected to be the areas which will help to lift the country out of its economic difficulties – but this will take some time.

Despite a roughly 50 per cent drop in the value of the króna between early 2008 and early 2009, on account of import taxes and high inflation (close to 20 per cent annually), the price tag for everything from beer to shoes in Reykjavik can leave visitors in a slight state of shock.

The city centre is full of art galleries, craft shops and clothing stores, despite the country's economic difficulties. Young Icelandic fashion designers also have their shops here. Bookshops are everywhere (an oft-cited fact is that Icelanders publish more books per capita than any other nation), selling photo books extolling the country alongside a limited supply of international newspapers and English-language titles.

Reykjavik has some first-rate museums, particularly relating to the history and fine art of the nation. Even though a small country, Iceland has its performing arts well represented. The main houses of the National Opera, National Theatre and Iceland Symphony Orchestra are all in the capital. Smaller and more off-the-cuff theatre groups pop up in various venues, and the legendary music scene uses the city's clubs and pubs as its exploratory workshops.

The city has a well-deserved reputation for being a party town. Cafés, clubs, pubs and restaurants stay open far into the night. Weekend closing hours are officially 05.00 or 06.00, although places remain buzzing until the party is over. The action doesn't start until around midnight, so friends stay at home, pre-party and delay forking out for highly taxed alcohol. If you go out to the bars before 22.00, it will only be you and the other tourists.

Visiting Reykjavik barely scratches the surface of seeing Iceland, but it's easy to view the country's extraordinary landscape by taking day trips from the capital. Beaches, geysers, glaciers, lakes, mountains, volcanic landscapes and waterfalls are all easily accessible.

When to go

Reykjavik literally lights up in the summer as its location, just below the Arctic Circle, means it never gets dark. This time of year is the most popular for visitors, as the temperatures are reasonable and the daylight virtually endless. Costs of hotels reflect this preference, and summer is the more expensive option in a two-season pricing system. Some (particularly budget) accommodation is available only during the months of June to September.

Alternatively, the winter, with its long nights, means that the *aurora borealis*, the spectacular Northern Lights show, is visible many evenings. Skiing is popular, especially in the north of the country, and sometimes even just outside Reykjavik. Festivals occur all year round, whether celebrating the arts, the changing of the seasons or simply just having a good time.

● *The summertime marathon brings the crowds out in force*

SEASONS & CLIMATE

Although it has the northernmost capital city in the world, Iceland is not as cold as the name implies. Surrounded by the Gulf Stream, a warm ocean current that comes from Florida, the climate is moderate all year long, being slightly warmer in the summer and a little colder in the winter.

Averages for Reykjavik are just below freezing in January and a little above 10°C (50°F) in the summer. Thermometers regularly record figures into the 20's C (70's F) during the warmer months, and t-shirt weather is not uncommon. During colder periods of the year, temperatures throughout the country vary more widely, and the further north one goes the colder it gets.

ANNUAL EVENTS

Reykjavik has events happening all year round. Celebrations are often planned for adjacent weekends, so that dates are not fixed from year to year. Check with the **tourist board** (Ⓦ www.visiticeland.com or Ⓦ www.visitreykjavik.is) for a more complete list and precise dates and times.

January–February
Þorrablót Take a chance and indulge in some of the country's weirder, more-or-less edible delicacies, including the legendary *hákarl* (rotten shark meat), during this traditional winter festival.
Winter Lights Festival Creating a glow in the darkness, this event promotes art projects focusing on the themes of light and energy. Ⓦ www.vetrarhatid.is
Food and Fun Here's an opportunity to taste gourmet cuisine, with the best of Iceland's chefs competing with their foreign counterparts. Ⓦ www.foodandfun.is

March–April

Bun Day & Bursting Day Just before Lent is Iceland's version
of Mardi Gras. The former encourages participants to stuff their
faces with cream buns, and the latter with more substantial fare
(salted meat and mushy peas).

First Day of Summer (third Thursday in April) Parades and street
entertainment celebrate the arrival of the summer season.

May–June

Reykjavik Arts Festival One of Iceland's most important cultural
festivals, this event has been held every May since 1970, and brings
together the best in local and international visual and performing
arts. Ⓦ www.artfest.is

Festival of the Sea Parades, arts, crafts, food and sailing competitions on
the first weekend in June commemorate the old Icelandic Seamen's Day.

Icelandic National Day A giant street party on 17 June, in celebration
of the granting of independence from Denmark in 1944. Festivities
last all day – a very long day indeed due to the midnight sun.

July–August

Gay Pride Rapidly becoming a tradition, this flamboyant festival
draws people from all over the world. Ⓦ www.gaypride.is

Culture Night & Marathon Virtually every gallery, museum,
restaurant, shop and business in Reykjavik opens its doors, presenting
free displays and performances. Beginning with several races of
different lengths, including a marathon, the day ends at midnight
with a massive firework display.

September–October

Reykjavik International Film Festival Films are screened in their original language in various locations around the city. Ⓦ www.riff.is

Reykjavik International Literature Festival A biennial festival in which both Icelandic and international authors present their books and participate in literary workshops. Ⓦ www.bokmenntahatid.is

Iceland Airwaves This rock and pop event takes place at various venues, including the Blue Lagoon (see page 106). Ⓦ www.icelandairwaves.com

November–December

31 December The firework display is legendary at this fantastic New Year's Eve celebration in a great party town.

PUBLIC HOLIDAYS
New Year's Day 1 Jan
Maundy Thursday 1 Apr 2010, 21 Apr 2011, 5 Apr 2012
Good Friday 2 Apr 2010, 22 Apr 2011, 6 Apr 2012
Easter Sunday 4 Apr 2010, 24 Apr 2011, 8 Apr 2012
Easter Monday 5 Apr 2010, 25 Apr 2011, 9 Apr 2012
First Day of Summer 15 Apr 2010, 21 Apr 2011, 19 Apr 2012
May Day 1 May
Ascension Day 13 May 2010, 2 June 2011, 17 May 2012
Whit Sunday 23 May 2010, 12 June 2011, 27 May 2012
Whit Monday 24 May 2010, 13 June 2011, 28 May 2012
National Day 17 June
Summer Bank Holiday 2 Aug 2010, 1 Aug 2011, 6 Aug 2012
Christmas Eve 24 Dec, public holiday from noon
Christmas Day 25 Dec
Boxing Day 26 Dec
New Year's Eve 31 Dec, public holiday from noon

Leaving the nest

Despite the North's reputation for frosty receptions, Reykjavik can get cosy fairly quickly. It begins on the plane, with Icelanders socialising with each other in the aisles, and continues as you bump into your flight companions during the first day downtown. You find a perfect café, become chummy with the barista, get sucked into a conversation with the locals in the hot pots, and soon you want to cancel that little trip you had planned and pool- and café-hop your week away.

You could, and it would be fun, but it would be a shame to miss out on what awaits you outside town. Iceland's natural landscape is famous for a reason: there is simply no other place like it. Its degree of emptiness and many moods awe even the hardest of urban hearts who take the time to venture into its depths. As any good Icelander will tell you, part of enjoying Reykjavik is enjoying its easy access to nature – rain or shine.

⬤ *Snæfellsnes Peninsula is only a two-hour drive from Reykjavik*

There are no trains in Iceland, which leaves you with two choices – bus or car (see Getting around, page 64). Buses will get you around the city, and tourist outfits will help you choose from a handful of tours that are all worthwhile for the first-time visitor. For a little off-the-beaten-track adventure that still gets you outside the city limits for a day trip, try taking a city bus to the foot of Mount Esja, the flat-topped mountain that looms over the bay. Conquering Esja is a popular weekend activity for city dwellers who like a challenging, two-hour uphill climb. A mellower physical option and a longer day starts with a bus in the other direction to the small town of Hveragerði, which has one of the city's best pools and a hot springs river behind town that you can walk to in about an hour, winter or summer. (Note: even though the trails are well marked, always check trail conditions with locals before you set off in winter, and let somebody know where you're heading whatever the season.)

If you have a driving licence and can afford it, hire a car. The Icelandic countryside is delightful, and if you stay off mountain paths, the roads are good and easy to navigate. Pull over to explore abandoned farmhouses, commune with Iceland's short, furry horses, check out waterfalls, and pause for hot dogs and ice cream at pit stops along the way. Legally, you are free to wander at will in Iceland, so the countryside is yours to explore, with the respect such civic trust deserves. For a day trip, head south to Vík and its stunning black sand beaches. For a longer journey, continue along the south coast to the incredibly diverse landscape that goes from pastoral to forlorn to sublime. Going north, take a spin around Snæfellsnes, a peninsula worth a weekend in itself, or drive up to Iceland's second city, Akureyri.

At the end of your trip, you'll roll back into Reykjavik and see how the city that you first thought was small suddenly feels alive with the energy of an international capital. Now you're really living like a local.

History

Iceland's story of discovery stems from traditional accounts, beginning with the Vikings in the ninth century. Naddoddur apparently lost his way while sailing to the Faeroe Islands and found himself in a country he named Snowland. He didn't stay for long, and neither did the Swede Garðar Svavarsson, who circumnavigated Iceland in 860 and spent the darker months at today's Húsavík. A Norwegian contemporary, Flóki Vilgerðarson, came here intending to settle, but the winter killed his livestock. He returned to his original home with tales of ice, and a new name for the country, Ísland (Iceland).

The medieval *Book of Settlements* continues the story, with Ingólfur Arnarson and his brother-in-law. Allegedly these two men had to give up their land in Norway as recompense for killing a nobleman's son, and they longed for the wide-open spaces described by Flóki. In 870, they set sail for the new land. The two men explored the country, and although his brother-in-law was eventually murdered by his own slaves, Ingólfur settled in 'Smoky Bay' – Reykja-vík – named for the distinctive plumes of smoke (wrongly identified pillars of steam). Iceland's original settlers were a combination of Norsemen and the Celtic slaves they brought from the British Isles.

Icelandic history is notable for the establishment of the world's first Parliament, the Alþingi, at Þingvellir in 930. The early 13th century was a time of violent action, with battles between various families and clans being waged almost non-stop for nearly 50 years. Finally, the Icelandic chieftains agreed to come under the rule of the King of Norway, thus ending the civil strife. By the beginning of the 15th century, the colonising country was devastated by a series of epidemics, including the Black Death. In Europe, Denmark took control of Sweden and Norway, and consequently Iceland came under the Danish crown.

For the next four hundred years, Iceland went through some of its hardest times as the nation was ravaged by disease and natural disasters.

However, in the 18th century, the establishment of *innréttingar* (workshops) provided the first hopes of modernisation. With Danish support, the Royal Treasurer, Skúli Magnússon, set up 'Enterprises' – a company whose aims were to instigate an economic rebirth in Iceland. Foreign craftsmen arrived in Reykjavik, and although fishing, agriculture, shipbuilding and sulphur mining were among the projects undertaken, wool working proved the most successful and lasted well into the 1800s. Much of the city's physical development stemmed from this period, yet only one building remains untouched: Aðalstraeti 10 is virtually original. In 1786, Reykjavik was granted town status.

The Alþingi was abolished in 1798, although by then it had long ceased to hold legislative powers and only controlled the judiciary, but in 1845 Denmark granted Iceland a certain degree of autonomy, and the Icelandic Parliament was reinstated. Previously isolated, Iceland's legalisation of free trade to all nations proved a turning point in the country's commercial development in 1855. Despite

◆ *Artefacts from the National Museum relate the city's history and traditions*

Reykjavik's long-standing official existence as a town, the first true council was set up in 1836.

World War I cut off almost all trade with Denmark, greatly aiding the independence struggle, and Iceland gained full autonomy in 1918. The next war also had a significant impact. In the spring of 1940, British troops occupied the country and Reykjavik's population nearly doubled with the addition of the UK military. The US took over in 1941 and unemployment disappeared virtually overnight. Following a referendum, Iceland declared independence from Denmark on 17 June 1944, with Sveinn Björnsson, acting Regent since 1940, elected as president.

Reykjavik embraced the future, becoming a modern city. A great deal of this forward thinking was due to new technology involving the harnessing of Iceland's vast hydroelectric and geothermal energy. Power was, and still is, produced cleanly and renewably: electricity via the plentiful water resources; heat from the country's thermal pools and springs. Some of the resulting revenue was channelled into the arts. The National Theatre began in 1950, as well as the Symphony Orchestra.

In the 1950s, Loftleiðir, now Icelandair, began transatlantic flights with a free stopover in Keflavík, Reykjavik's airport. This brought in a globetrotting public, and helped overcome the Icelanders' sense of isolation from the outside world. The city breaks continue to this day.

Modern-day Iceland is increasingly tied into the global economy. In 2003, huge deals involving aluminium trading gave the economy a boost and the private financial sector exploded. In the autumn of 2008, however, Iceland became one of the first victims of the global financial crisis. As the nation's debt, inflation and unemployment levels spiralled, Reyjavikers took to the streets in protest. The challenges that face the country today are by no means small, but a feeling of optimism remains that, in the end, the country will emerge from its economic quagmire stronger than ever.

THE WESTMANN ISLANDS

In November 1963, just off the south coast of Iceland and close to the major fishing port of the Vestmannaeyjar Islands (Westmann Islands), fishermen noticed the first rumblings of an offshore volcano. For three and a half years the eruption continued, and when the flow finally stopped, a land mass rising 169 m (555 ft) out of the sea had been created. The island was named Surtsey, after Surtur, a fire-wielding Norse god. Even before the lava cooled, Surtsey had been declared an area of special scientific interest and off limits to casual human visitors, so that scientists could study implantation methods and bird migration patterns of the newest island on earth. Today, plants have taken root and several bird species nest here. The island was designated a UNESCO World Heritage Site in 2008.

Just under ten years later, on 23 January 1973, a huge fissure opened suddenly and unexpectedly, close to the main Westmann Islands' town of Heimaey. A mass evacuation commenced, with people hurriedly being flown and shipped over to the mainland. Two months later, the fire brigade installed a series of pipes and hoses so that the encroaching lava, which threatened to block the country's most productive southern port, could be diverted away from the mouth of the harbour. In July the eruption halted, with the island almost 30 per cent larger than it had been in January, and nearly half the town covered with volcanic material. The re-channelled lava made the harbour better than ever.

Lifestyle

Despite the economic crash of 2008, Reykjavikers still live relatively well. The city is small yet boasts almost every major European store. Designer shops and art galleries may not be as frequented by the locals as they once were, and sales of wool for knitting and 'traditional' Icelandic foods like horsemeat may have increased, but there are no shortages in shops or restaurants and visitors are unlikely to notice any difference in lifestyle from other Western

⬤ *Relaxing in hot pots and spas is all part of the local lifestyle*

European communities. In any case, many of Reykjavik's greatest attractions are completely free: its relative lack of pollution, its cleansing rain and pure air, its beautiful mountain and sea vistas and its general atmosphere of healthiness.

When you do have to get your wallet out, however, you'll rapidly come down to earth. Iceland varies from being expensive to very expensive, depending on the exchange rate. Although the króna lost about 50 per cent of its value in the months following the 2008 financial crisis, inflation rapidly caught up and prices remain only slightly lower for visitors than they were during previous years. Alcohol and petrol are particularly pricey due to high government taxes – partly as a disincentive, and partly to raise state revenue. Petrol prices are also inflated due to the cost of importing it. Most people own cars, although there are fewer 'gas guzzling' four-wheel drives now than previously. Alcohol, on the other hand, is still drunk widely despite the high cost, with more and more people saving money by purchasing bottles from the national wine shop and drinking at home rather than frequenting pubs.

Salaries are high, but not in proportion to the additional costs, and during the recession, many employers have frozen or even lowered wages in an effort to avoid making redundancies. Income tax is also considerable, although this does mean that services such as healthcare and education are virtually free. Many Icelanders cope by taking on more than one job, often more than two. Sometimes the occupations have nothing to do with each other, such as an industrial consultant who also runs owner-operated SuperJeep tours or an actor who also escorts camping groups. The locals themselves admit that life is expensive, and given high inflation and rising debts (mortgages and loans are tied to inflation), sometimes a second job is more of an obligation than a choice.

Culture

For such a small city, Reykjavik has a very large number of cultural venues. The Listasafn Íslands (National Gallery) holds the main collection of Icelandic art, as well as some 19th- and 20th-century examples. Kjarvalsstaðir presents the work of one of the most popular landscape painters, Jóhannes Kjarval, while the Ásmundarsafn exhibits Ásmundur Sveinsson's sculptures in his extraordinary house. More radical modern art is shown at the multi-functional Hafnarhúsið, and the Sigurjón Ólafsson Museum is in the artist's own studio. The Árbæjarsafn is the city's outdoor assembly of historic buildings, mostly from central Reykjavik, gathered in a semi-rural area of fields and farms, not far from the centre. The Þjóðmenningarhúsið (Culture House) is home to some original medieval manuscripts of the Icelandic sagas as well as some changing exhibitions.

The jewel in the city's cultural crown is the Þjóðminjasafn Íslands (National Museum of Iceland). State of the art, with beautifully presented displays (and an excellent coffee house), the museum describes the country's history.

Smaller, private galleries abound, with artists exhibiting their own work. The main shopping street, Laugavegur, contains several of them. Nearby, Skólavorðustígur, punctuated by the dramatic Hallgrímskirkja at the top of the street, is developing a reputation as something of an 'art' street, with painting, ceramic and fabric stores lining its pavements.

Reykjavik has a National Opera, Symphony Orchestra and Theatre each performing regularly, although the number of events increases

---

▶ *The majestic interior of Hallgrimskirkja is just the venue for musical events*

ADMISSION CHARGES

All of the museums and pools listed in this guide charge admission unless otherwise stated, although you can get free entry to several of these with the Reykjavik Welcome Card. Some museums also have one day a week with free admission: the day varies from place to place, so call or check the website to find out which day it is. Live music in pubs and clubs is generally free but you are expected to buy a drink.

outside the summer tourist season. Iceland has a thriving music scene, with an extraordinary number of both professional and amateur jazz and rock groups featured in clubs and pubs.

Reykjavik is also home to the National Opera, National Theatre and Iceland Symphony Orchestra, each of which performs regularly throughout the year. The city opens up its galleries, museums, music and theatrical venues, and impromptu performers do their thing(s) from early morning till long past midnight. Other happenings on the annual calendar include festivals that celebrate sacred arts, dance, tango, literature, film, jazz, rock and pop and most other forms of entertainment. Even Hallgrímskirkja, Reykjavik's logo and unmistakeable icon, shows off its acoustics with the occasional concert.

◉ *Early morning at Hallgrímskirkja*

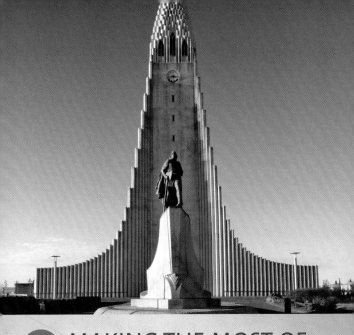

MAKING THE MOST OF
Reykjavik

Shopping

The sense of Reykjavik being small, yet having virtually everything one could want, extends to its shopping. The city centre is full of delightful boutiques, craft shops, fine fashion venues, souvenir stalls and even convenience food markets. Slightly further afield are huge shopping malls with international brand-name as well as Icelandic specialist stores. There is even a huge weekend flea market for bargains and offbeat items.

Laugavegur is central Reykjavik's most prominent street and its prime shopping area. Narrow, so that cars have to drive slowly, it feels almost like a pedestrian precinct. Shops line its entire length, the slightly downmarket and funkier ones further away from the centre, the more exclusive ones highly visible closer to the city's heart. Much of the street's focus is on clothing. At the financially (but not physically) lower end of the street, it's possible to find second-hand goods and quirky items appealing to a younger crowd. As the street continues, the fashion becomes more exotic, with Icelandic design and one-off items being sold. Side lanes begin to branch off, with exclusive fashion and jewellery sandwiched between fine art galleries. Dropping down in the direction of the harbour, brand names such as Prada begin to appear among the cafés (great for a break among all this commerce). 66° North, Iceland's high-quality weather gear producer, has one of its more prominent show stores here.

Once near the main square, the one-off shops disappear and are replaced by souvenir venues, offering mostly Icelandic woollen goods. It's possible to pick up cheaper – and less practical – goods,

▶ *Kringlan Mall offers every retail experience the visitor could want*

such as toy puffins, 'Iceland' t-shirts and photography books, sometimes on sale.

Bookshops are scattered along the length of the shopping streets, and they also sell foreign newspapers. Books are sold in several languages, but English titles dominate the non-Icelandic publications.

Further away are the huge shopping malls. Kringlan Mall, located near the geographical, if not tourist, centre of greater Reykjavik, is an archetypal centre with 150 shops and restaurants. Also here are

● A Viking helmet may be just the souvenir for you to take home

USEFUL SHOPPING PHRASES

What time do the shops open/close?
Hvenær opnar/lokar?
Kvenaier opnar/lohkar?

How much is it?
Hvað kostar þetta?
Kvahth kostahr thetta?

I'd like to buy ...
Mig langar að kaupa ...
Mikh lowngar ath koipah ...

pharmacies, banks, doctors' offices, a food court and a multi-screen movie theatre. Smaralind, the largest shopping centre in Iceland, is in Kopavogur, close enough to Reykjavik to be accessible by public transport and conveniently on the way to Keflavik airport. The mall has the usual shops and businesses as well as a huge hypermarket, Hagkaup.

At weekends, Reykjavik's flea market down by the harbour, Kolaportið, comes to life. A huge warehouse full of second-hand clothing, rock memorabilia, book stores and kitsch items, the market is a popular place to stroll among Reykjavik's cast-offs. In the back is a section for strange Icelandic food specialities, including salt fish, *harðfiskur* (dried fish which the locals eat like crisps) and even *hákarl*, the rotten shark speciality bearable only with a shot of *brennivín*, the high-octane Icelandic spirit.

Eating & drinking

What Reykjavik lacks in inexpensive options for eating, it virtually overcompensates for in gastronomic variety. The choice of restaurants, cafés, bistros, bars, pubs and even fast-food outlets is huge, especially for what seems to be such a small city. Most tastes and nationalities are catered for, with American, Asian, Danish, French, Italian and vegetarian venues especially well covered. Of course, Icelandic cuisine is highly regarded, with the excellent resources of fish, seafood and lamb being featured. It's possible to save money by visiting the local supermarkets for picnic lunch foods and between-meal snacks, although prices here are also fairly high. Try to avoid the convenience stores and aim for the proper food stores.

Many restaurants are open all day from about 11.00 to late in the evening. Other restaurants close after lunch and then re-open for dinner at around 18.00. Closing times are dependent on how busy the restaurant is, and final orders can sometimes be very late indeed. At weekends and at peak times of the year, such as during festivals or on public holidays, it is advisable to reserve a table at a restaurant well in advance.

PRICE CATEGORIES
The restaurant price guides used in the book indicate the approximate cost of a three-course meal for one person, excluding drinks, at the time of writing.
£ up to 3,500Kr.   ££ 3,500–6,500Kr.   £££ over 6,500Kr.

● *Seafood – of all shapes and sizes – is a staple of the local cuisine*

Eating out is expensive everywhere, although this is one thing that has become relatively cheaper for visitors with foreign currency. Quality is generally extremely high. Fine cuisine is the standard, and once the shock of seeing the cost on the menu, let alone later on the final bill, is overcome, the experience is a pleasure. Tipping is not part of local custom, and never done. Locals dress well and this fashion consciousness is reflected in their evening attire, although dress codes are not usually enforced in restaurants. If diners appear at the door in jeans and hiking boots, they will not be turned away, but will definitely be identified as tourists.

Cafés are an essential part of Reykjavik life to both the locals and tourists. It's possible to order a cafetière or designer latte and spend hours in one place, sipping that long-deserved cup of coffee, conducting business or merely people-watching. Many of the city's cafés are chameleons, serving java, then food, and then becoming clubs in the evening. This transition can happen non-stop, with service and customers slipping almost seamlessly into the next phase. Coffee houses that really do specialise in coffee tend to start early and close around 18.00. Cafés usually open around 11.00 and close when they want, around 01.00 on weekdays and up to 06.00 at weekends.

If you think the food at an Icelandic restaurant is expensive, wait until you see the prices on the drinks menu. Alcohol is particularly expensive, with a bottle of house wine at a restaurant regularly costing over 4,000Kr. Tap water, thankfully, is free and tasty. Nevertheless, ordering drinks to accompany a meal is fairly common; people in Reykjavik enjoy their wine with dinner. Clubs and pubs serve beverages at the same prices, and do good business.

◗ *A bar in central Reykjavik awaits the crowds*

Locals often start early, purchasing their bottles at the state-run off-licences called Vínbúð, and beginning their drinking at home.

When both your wallet and your stomach decide they've had enough of eating out in restaurants, don't despair. Reykjavik has a high number of takeaway and fast-food eateries. Names such as Domino's, Kentucky Fried Chicken, McDonald's and Pizza Hut are familiar, while the Icelandic equivalents are just as prevalent. Be careful, though, as a McDonald's meal can still be quite pricey. Pizza, for some unexplained reason, is particularly expensive, with a meal and a cola creeping into the **££** category. The city's best food bargain is a *pylsa (*hot dog) and it's possible to find a decent one for less than 300Kr. – about £1.50.

Buying food at supermarkets is a reasonable option, particularly away from the city centre. Convenience stores such as 10-11 are just that, with long hours and good locations, but their prices are comparatively high. Larger supermarkets, such as Bónus and Hagkaup, are better value but harder to find. Street markets offer quality and organic produce and as such cost a bit more.

Enough talking about prices: now let's talk about taste. Iceland is justly proud of some of its local food, particularly fish and lamb. The former is often found as salt fish, the dried then reconstituted chunk of cod that is found in many regional dishes. Lamb, too, is delicious, and can be eaten economically in the traditional hearty meat and vegetable soup common at lunch (and especially good on those cold, wet days).

Seabirds are fairly common on the menu, with puffin being the most prevalent. Often served smoked, the taste has been compared to veal. More fun, however, are the weird, uniquely Icelandic dishes sold mostly at speciality restaurants. *Hákarl* is putrefied shark meat, served in tiny chunks, and virtually inedible. It smells horrible,

USEFUL DINING PHRASES

I would like a table for ... people
Get ég fengið borð fyrir ...
Get yehkh fengith borth feerir ...

May I see the menu?
Get ég fengið að sjá matseðilinn?
Get yehkh fengith ahth syow mahtsethilin?

I am a vegetarian
Ég er grænmetisæta
Yehkh ehr grain-maytisaitah

Where is the lavatory (restroom)?
Hvar er klósettið?
Kvar er klosetith?

May I have the bill?
Get ég fengið reikninginn?
Get yehkh fengith raykningin?

but tastes worse, and is usually consumed with generous portions of *brennivín*, a powerful and taste-numbing spirit. Pickled ram's testicles, served commonly as a sort of pâté, and cod chins or cheeks, taken from the fish's head, are legacies from the days when almost anything was considered edible.

Entertainment & nightlife

Despite the high cost of alcohol and food, Reykjavik is justifiably proud of its legendary bar, club and pub nightlife. As with most of the city's commodities, the number of such venues is disproportionately high for such a small population. The inhabitants like to party. Most of the action happens at weekends, when the bars close at 03.00, 04.00, 05.00 or even later, depending on how the party is going (on weekdays, places close around 01.00). Nothing much really happens until midnight, when some clubs and bars begin to charge an entry fee. To avoid the payment, arrive early, brave the lack of action, and hang out until things get going. The clubs will not ask for money, nor throw out sitting clientele.

The secret to the festivities is to choose the right place. The bars that are in vogue change on a regular basis and what is 'in' one month will not necessarily be 'the' place the next. Check the monthly guides to see the trends, or ask the locals. Places are generally geared to particular criteria; for example, age, dress, locals, tourists, food, music, drinking, chat, meeting others or simply hanging out with friends. It's a sophisticated system.

Generally, locals go home after work and relax a bit, giving them the opportunity to dress up before going out. They often begin their alcohol consumption at home where it's cheaper, or at informal gatherings at friends' houses. By the time they reach the bar, the initial drinking is done, so that the high cost of alcohol isn't so damaging. Nevertheless, the locals party hard, and prices don't diminish consumption. Favourite places are often chosen by who the Reykjavikers think will be where. The city is small, and most

● *The Kaffibarrin (see page 86) is one of Reykjavik's most popular bars*

YOUR FRIEND FOR THE NIGHT

If the prospect of trying to break into the club scene is a bit intimidating, especially for a short break, 'Your Reykjavik Nightlife Friend' could be a help. A legitimate tour guide, Jón Kári Hilmarsson offers a quick entry into Reykjavik's night-time party life. He seems to know practically everyone in the city and has his finger on the pulse of where the hotspots are, making him the perfect guide to a night on the town.

Recommended by the tourist board, Jón Kári meets his clients ahead of time to see what they would like and then shows them around to places he feels are appropriate. Contact 'Your Reykjavik Nightlife Friend' on ☎ 822 6600 ⓦ www.nightlifefriend.is

people know each other, as is evident by the handshakes and rousing hellos that greet arrivals. Foreigners can be welcomed, or ignored, depending on various things, such as how tight the regular group is, how well the visitors are dressed, how open both the locals and visitors are, or any number of reasons. In general, people are friendly, although they can be a little aloof.

If you prefer classical music, cinema and the performing arts to thumping music and non-stop drinking, you're in luck. Despite the reputation for clubbing, Reykjavik has good cultural alternatives for night-time entertainment. The City Theatre (see page 104) and National Theatre (see page 87) are professional companies that put on regular productions. There are several other theatre groups offering performances, some in English.

As well as rock bands and jazz groups, the **National Opera** (ⓐ Ingólfsstræti 2A ❶ 511 4200 Ⓦ www.opera.is) and the **Iceland Symphony Orchestra** (ⓐ Háskólabíó (University Cinema on Hagatorg) ❶ 545 2500 Ⓦ www.sinfonia.is) offer more formal musical opportunities.

Cinema is popular too, with most films shown in their original language. US and UK movies, except those for children, are not usually dubbed. For more information on cinemas, visit Ⓦ www.kvikmyndir.is and click 'í bíó' for film times and locations.

It's worth doing some research into what's on during your stay in the city and, for some popular concerts or festivals, booking tickets in advance. There is no shortage of information on Reykjavik. Most accessible is the website for the **Reykjavik Tourist Board** (Ⓦ www.visitreykjavik.is) which includes up-to-date listings. Tourist booklets, such as *Reykjavik City Guide* (Ⓦ www.icelandtoday.is) and *What's On in Reykjavik* (Ⓦ www.whatson.is), are updated monthly.

The street mag, the *Reykjavik Grapevine* (Ⓦ www.grapevine.is) is very useful. General Icelandic publications updated seasonally, such as the *Visitor's Guide* (Ⓦ www.visitorsguide.is), are also extremely helpful.

Sport & relaxation

SPECTATOR SPORTS

The two main sports that Reykjavikers like to watch are football and handball. Iceland has produced a surprisingly good football team, with a following as enthusiastic as any other in Europe. Handball, too, gets a good crowd and the men's team won a silver medal in the sport at the 2008 Beijing Olympics.

Both these disciplines hold their games at the main sports stadium in Laugardalur Valley (see page 88). For more information regarding dates and times, contact the tourist board. An interesting fact for chess fans is that the Laugardalshöll sports hall hosted the famous 1972 World Chess Championship between the Russian grandmaster Boris Spassky and the American Bobby Fischer.

PARTICIPATION & RELAXATION

Laugardalur Valley (see page 88) is the centre of many of Reykjavik's sporting activities, not only for professional teams but also for amateur enthusiasts. As well as including running tracks, football fields and an indoor ice rink, there are also the largest thermal pool and gym in the city, as well as an upmarket spa.

Angling is very popular, although it can be extremely expensive. Salmon fishing is one of Iceland's largest tourist revenue earners. Despite the fact that the best rivers are outside the city and have to be booked years in advance, fish have been caught in the Elliðaár river that runs through Reykjavik. Trout-fishing permits are available for a small fee, and can be used in lakes throughout Iceland.

There are five golf courses in the Reykjavik area, often with lava-strewn greens or picturesque sea views. See ⓦ www.golf.is or call ⓣ 514 4050 for information and locations. The best-known venue,

SPA CITY

One of the resources upon which Iceland sits, the natural hot springs generated by volcanic activity, has been harnessed to create a favourite national pastime – sitting in geothermal waters. Although some in the country are naturally occurring, in Reykjavik what appear to be swimming pools are actually comfortably heated thermal pools. Alongside are 'hot pots', or whirlpool-like baths. Traditionally, locals can spend hours here. The pools are popular winter and summer, and are surprisingly inexpensive (and included in the Reykjavik Card).

A very precise etiquette accompanies the use of spa pools. Entrants are required to shower thoroughly with soap beforehand without a swimsuit in order to ensure the hygiene of the pool itself, then put the suit back on before entering the water. There are seven of these public pools in Reykjavik. For information, visit 🕲 www.spacity.is

however, is in the northern city of Akureyri, where the all-night **Arctic Open** (🕲 www.arcticopen.is) is held on the summer solstice, in virtual 24-hour daylight.

Iceland is a hikers' paradise, with many of the best areas reached on a day trip from the city. Locally, the best bet for a good stiff climb is to walk up Mt Esja, the mountain that faces Reykjavik from across the bay. It takes from 1–3 hours to reach the summit at 900 m (2,700 ft) above sea level. From the centre of Reykjavik, take bus 15 to Mosfellsbær (a town just to the northeast), then transfer to bus 57 to reach the foot of the mountain.

Horse-riding excursions are very popular, particularly on the

● *The Icelandic horse has a placid nature – great for novice riders*

unique Icelandic horses. An ancient breed, they have two special gaits, including a running walk – the *tölt* – that is particularly suited to riding long trails. Based in the city, tours are offered in the nearby countryside. **Laxnes Horse Farm** (❶ 566 6179 ⓦ www.laxnes.is) is one reliable company, but there are several others. Check with the tourist office for details.

Glacier excursions on skidoos, which are one-person snowmobiles or motorised sleds, are available all year round. Day trips are available from **Activity Group** (ⓦ www.activity.is), **Reykjavik Excursions** (ⓦ www.re.is), **Iceland Excursions** (ⓦ www.icelandexcursions.is) and **Mountain Taxi** (ⓦ www.mountaintaxi.is), among others.

Skiing is a popular sport in Iceland, and from November to April, if there is good snow, two ski resorts operate around Reykjavik: Bláfjöll and Skálafell. However, most people head north to the winter sports area of **Akureyri** (W www.hlidarfjall.is), where snow is more likely and the facilities are better.

Whale-watching has arrived in Reykjavik, and seagoing excursions are available to see humpback, minke and orca whales as well as dolphins, puffins and seals. What is actually viewed – no guarantees are made – depends on the season. Tours operated by **Elding Whale Watching** (W www.elding.is) leave from the Old Harbour. Further north, in Húsavík, the 'Whale Watching Capital of Europe', there is a 98 per cent record of sea mammal viewing when the boats go out. Here, **North Sailing** (W www.nordursigling.is) and **Gentle Giants** (W www.gentlegiants.is) are the companies that sail.

● *A whale-watching trip may be a rewarding experience...*

Accommodation

Reykjavik is pricey and the cost of accommodation is no exception, especially since many hotels now charge in euros rather than krónur. However, the standard of facilities, cleanliness and hospitality is generally high. Neighbouring communities have less expensive guesthouses, although the number of these outlying places to stay is quite limited and the locations comparatively far from the centre. Within central Reykjavik, accommodation is plentiful.

Watch out for festivals and special events, when spaces are filled very quickly (by out-of-town Icelanders, as well as foreign tourists). It's wise to book well ahead in such cases. The tourist board online, at Ⓦ www.visitreykjavik.is, has a comprehensive listing with excellent links to the individual lodgings.

Despite the tourist board's successful attempts to introduce Reykjavik as a low-season winter, as well as a high-season summer, destination, rates drop as much as 25 per cent from October to April. Prices are generally two-tier, with hotel stays in the colder months proving to be much more affordable. Unless travelling with a group or on a package tour, discounts are not generally offered for longer durations. Breakfast is almost always included.

Guesthouses offer a more intimate and personable alternative

PRICE CATEGORIES

All are approximate prices for a single night in a double room for two people during the summer season (May–September). Note that many hotels now charge in euros.

£ up to 15,000Kr.   ££ 15,000–25,000Kr.   £££ over 25,000Kr.

to the bigger and smarter hotels, although the price difference isn't always a great deal. Like bed & breakfasts, which are cheaper, it's a good way to get to know a few more Reykjavikers. Many guesthouses have shared bathroom facilities. Some even offer dorm rooms and kitchen areas to reduce living costs still further.

Reykjavik has a campsite and two youth hostels, and there is another hostel and campsite in nearby Hafnarfjörður. In the capital, the hostels are located in the Laugardalur Valley, a bus ride from the centre, and on Vesturgata, close to the Tourist Information Centre. Prices here are not as low as one would expect, and visitors often prefer the convenience, and not much higher cost, of staying in a dorm room in a guesthouse in town.

HOTELS

Home Luxury Apartments ££ A newer addition to Reykjavik's increasing trove of upscale digs for travellers, the Home apartments are sleek, modern studios and a penthouse, with décor by Icelandic artists – essentially a small design hotel in an historic downtown house. The penthouse is a real splurge, complete with a gourmet kitchen and a teak bath. ⓐ Skólastræti 1, 101 (Inner city & harbour) ⓣ 896 5665 ⓦ www.homereykjavik.is

Hótel Björk ££ This affordable – by Reykjavik standards – hotel has all basic facilities and is part of the quality Kea chain. ⓐ Brautarholt 22–24, 105 (Beyond the centre) ⓣ 511 3777 ⓦ www.keahotels.is

Hótel Frón ££ This renovated apartment hotel is situated on Laugavegur, the city's main shopping street. ⓐ Laugavegur 22A, 101 (Inner city & harbour) ⓣ 511 4666 ⓦ www.hotelfron.is

Hótel Klöpp ££ A modern and basic place to stay, right off the main drag, that leaves some cash in your pocket. @ Klapparstígur 26, 101 (Inner city & harbour) ❶ 595 8520 Ⓦ www.centerhotels.com

Hótel Leifur Eiríksson ££ Under the shadow of Hallgrímskirkja, the city's dominant building, the small and friendly Leifur Eiríksson has nicely furnished rooms. @ Skólavörðustígur 45, 101 (Inner city & harbour) ❶ 562 0800 Ⓦ www.hotelleifur.is

🔽 *The original art deco style of Hótel Borg is still evident*

Luna Hotel Apartments ££–£££ In an ideal spot in Reykjavik's historic 101 neighbourhood, this apartment hotel is ideal if you want to feel like you're living the Icelandic life. ⓐ Spítalastígur 1, 101 (Inner city & harbour) ❶ 511 2800 ⓦ www.luna.is

101 hotel £££ Standard features such as under-floor heating and walk-in showers demonstrate the luxury at this centrally-located hotel, where modernity and comfort combine immaculately. ⓐ Hverfisgata 10, 101 (Inner city & harbour) ❶ 580 0101 ⓦ www.101hotel.is

Hótel Borg £££ Dominating Austurvöllur Square, the 80-year-old Hótel Borg has long been a central Reykjavik landmark. Since its opening, this hotel has been the place to stay, whether for visiting dignitaries or for the more affluent tourist who wants a true urban Icelandic experience. Although retaining the art deco style that was the height of fashion when it was built, the hotel has 21st century facilities and all modern comforts. ⓐ Pósthússtræti 11, 101 (Inner city & harbour) ❶ 551 1440 ⓦ www.hotelborg.is

Hótel Óðinsve £££ A 4-star hotel in the centre of Reykjavik's 101 neighbourhood, Óðinsve has tastefully decorated rooms and two restaurants: the celebrated Siggi Hall and more casual Brauðbær. ⓐ Þórsgata 1, 101 (Inner city & harbour) ❶ 511 6200 ⓦ www.hotelodinsve.is

Hótel Þingholt £££ Following in the footsteps of design hotels in Europe, the 52-room Hótel Þingholt boasts trendy décor and an even trendier restaurant and bar. ⓐ Þingholtsstræti 3–5, 101 (Inner city & harbour) ❶ 595 8530 ⓦ www.centerhotels.com

GUESTHOUSES

Adam Guesthouse £ Rooms are equipped with bathrooms, basic kitchens and free internet, and are situated on the 'art street'.
ⓐ Skólavörðustígur 42, 101 (Inner city & harbour) ⓣ 896 0242
ⓦ www.adamhotel.com

Domus Guesthouse £ In an old building in the heart of the centre, Domus has 12 double rooms, plentiful dorm space, three studio apartments and a shared kitchen. ⓐ Hverfisgata 45, 101 (Inner city & harbour) ⓣ 561 1200 ⓦ www.domusguesthouse.is

Flóki Guesthouse £ Slightly off the beaten track, this friendly guesthouse is still close to most of what the city has to offer.
ⓐ Flókagata 1, 105 (Beyond the centre) ⓣ 552 1155
ⓦ www.hotelfloki.is

● *If you want a cheaper option, consider sleeping-bag accomodation*

Guesthouse 101 £ With spacious rooms and shared facilities, this modern guesthouse is located on the main shopping street. ⓐ Laugavegur 101, 101 (Inner city & harbour) ⓣ 562 6101 ⓦ www.iceland101.com

Guesthouse Butterfly £ Friendly and welcoming, this intimate guesthouse a short stroll from the centre offers just six rooms, two apartments, and a communal kitchen. It's only open in summer. ⓐ Ránargata 8A, 101 (Inner city & harbour) ⓣ 894 1864 ⓦ www.kvasir.is

Guesthouse Ísafold £ Well placed in old – and quieter – Reykjavik, Ísafold is still close to the best of the city's activities. ⓐ Bárugata 11, 101 (Inner city & harbour) ⓣ 561 2294 ⓦ www.isafoldguesthouse.is

Kríunes Guesthouse £ Further away and close to Lake Elliðavatn, this virtual mansion blends the quiet of the countryside with relative proximity to the capital. ⓐ við Vatnsenda, 203 Kópavogur (Beyond the centre) ⓣ 567 2245 ⓦ www.kriunes.is

Reykjavik City Hostel £ A bus ride from the centre, this popular hostel in the Laugardalur Valley is always crowded in summer – perhaps as it's next door to the city's biggest pool. If you prefer to be closer to the centre, try its sister hostel on Vesturgata (ⓣ 553 8120). ⓐ Sundlaugavegur 34, 105 (Beyond the centre) ⓣ 553 8110 ⓦ www.hostel.is

Salvation Army Guesthouse £ Incredibly situated right in the heart of town, this guesthouse has rooms for one to five people as well as sleeping-bag accommodation. ⓐ Kirkjustræti 2, 101 (Inner city & harbour) ⓣ 561 3203 ⓦ www.guesthouse.is

THE BEST OF REYKJAVIK

Whether you are on a flying visit to Reykjavik or have a little
more time to explore the city and its surroundings, there are
some sights, places and experiences that you should not miss.
For the best attractions for children, see page 149.

TOP 10 ATTRACTIONS

- **Laugavegur** The city's main shopping street is lined with
  picturesque shops and houses (see page 72)

- **Hallgrímskirkja** A church disguised as a space ship is the city's
  most recognisable landmark (see page 72)

- **Þjóðminjasafn Íslands (National Museum of Iceland)** A fine,
  state-of-the-art museum, with exhibits describing anything
  anyone could ever want to know about the history of the
  country (see page 77)

- **Þjóðmenningarhúsið (The Culture House)** Superb original
  medieval manuscripts of the Icelandic Sagas are displayed
  within this city-centre museum (see page 77)

- **Whale-watching and puffin tours** Magnificent giant mammals and comic, colourful birds can be spotted while cruising Reykjavik's beautiful bay (see page 41)

- **Café society** Whether sitting outside on a warm day, or inside on a cold one, coffee-drinking and people-watching are national hobbies (see page 30)

- **Thermal pools** Natural geothermal energy heats these public swimming pools and provides an inexpensive and delightful spa experience (see page 39)

- **Pub and club culture** Find out what makes Reykjavik's nightlife so legendary (see page 34)

- **Festivals** Art, culture, food and historical festivals occur throughout the year (see page 9)

- **Nature at the door** Much of Iceland's spectacular scenery is available a mere day trip away (see page 106)

◯ *Skógafoss waterfall in the south of Iceland*

Suggested itineraries

HALF-DAY: REYKJAVIK IN A HURRY

Stroll down Laugavegur, perusing the quirkier shops at the more downmarket end and admiring the fine art and design as the route approaches the city's centre. Perhaps stop at one of the main coffee houses, Kaffitár or Café Sólon for example, on the way. Continue to the Old Harbour and view the fishing boats. Turn back and walk through the Old Town, or through Austurvöllur Square, the city's traditional heart. Walk towards the modern Ráðhúsið (City Hall), maybe stepping inside to see the free exhibition. Continue along the banks of the Tjörnin (City Pond) to enjoy the fine views and feed the ducks.

1 DAY: TIME TO SEE A LITTLE MORE

With a bit more time, visit one or more of the museums, some worth a whole day to themselves. The National Museum is excellent for Iceland's history, while the Culture House shows off original medieval manuscripts.

Reykjavik also has several fine art galleries, which are certainly worth viewing. Kjarvalsstaðir and the more modern Hafnarhúsið and Ásmundarsafn Sculpture Garden together make up what is known as the Reykjavik Art Gallery; all have free admission.

During the season, whale-watching is a great way to spend an afternoon – on a calm day! An excellent way to finish off the afternoon is by visiting one of Reykjavik's seven thermal pools, all open to the public.

2–3 DAYS: TIME TO SEE MUCH MORE

For longer stays, investing in a Reykjavik Welcome Card (available for

24-, 48- or 72-hour durations) is a good idea, as it provides entry to most of the city's museums and swimming pools, as well as free transport on the buses. A morning to spare might be worth allowing for recovery from the previous night's indulgence in Reykjavik's pub and club life.

One day should certainly be spent on an excursion to some of the country's incredible scenic spots. The Golden Circle tour includes the historic and geological site of Þingvellir, the erupting hot springs of Geysir and the beautiful Gullfoss waterfall, and can be visited by organised tour or rental car.

Alternatively, an easier day can be spent at the Blue Lagoon resort, a gigantic hot spring pool fed by a geothermal power station's run-off.

LONGER: ENJOYING REYKJAVIK TO THE FULL

There are so many festivals happening in Reykjavik that an extended stay is bound to overlap some event. Find time to go for a performance by the National Opera, National Theatre or Iceland Symphony Orchestra. In addition, the city is an excellent base for exploring the rest of Iceland, with several tour companies offering both single- and multi-day tours.

Snæfellsjökull, the glacier-capped mountain often visible in the distance across Faxaflói Bay, is excellent as a destination for both one- and multi-day trips. A short flight, or longer drive, to Akureyri provides an excellent two-day (or more) option, as there are many extraordinary scenic spots within easy reach of Iceland's second city.

Something for nothing

Despite Reykjavik's often justified reputation for being expensive, the city is not unfriendly to those visitors who have little cash to spare. There are quite a few things to see and do that require no funds at all. Although the city limits encompass a large area, central Reykjavik is quite small, and most things to see are within walking distance. Probably the most fun thing to do is stroll, looking at the city's outdoor architecture and shop windows. If hunger strikes, though not quite free, *pylsa* (hot dogs) from street stands are inexpensive and provide enough strength to continue the free tour. *Skyr*, Iceland's unique, yogurt-like dairy product, is also a cheap protein source. In the very centre is the City Hall, a modern building partially sitting astride the City Pond. There are often exhibitions

● *Relaxation and recreation at Nauthólsvík*

here and a fascinating giant relief map of the country. At weekends, the indoor Kolaportið Market, down by the harbour, is a huge flea market selling lots of weird and wonderful things, including old rock memorabilia, obscure Icelandic books and some of the country's more questionable gastronomic specialities.

Hallgrímskirkja is free and is open most of the day (although the climb to the top of the 75 m (250 ft) viewpoint incurs a small fee). The massive city church is an intriguing place to visit and it is sometimes possible to sit in on concert rehearsals.

Two museums, the National Gallery and Ásmundarsafn, offer free entry to both their interior collections and their outdoor sculpture gardens. Norræna Húsið (Nordic House), which explains Nordic cultures to locals as well as visitors, offers free entry to its exhibition hall. The Reykjavik Museum of Photography also invites people in without charge. Perlan (the Pearl) in Öskjuhlíð Hill is closer than it looks from town, and is a fairly easy walk. Entry to this complex, partially constructed from six hot-water storage tanks, is free to the public, and a walk up to the top floor will provide one of the best views over the city. Just outside the Pearl is Strokkur, an artificial copy of one of the country's more impressive geysers. Further down the hill and past the domestic airport is a recreation area that includes Nauthólsvík, the outdoor sand beach that has been roped off so that the water within is geothermally heated. On warm days the place is buzzing.

Somewhat of a walk is Kringlan, Reykjavik's giant shopping mall. Full of mainstream shops, food halls and lots of people, it's still a fun place to hang out if money is short. If the timing is right, many of the festivals are giant street parties, and with luck, music, performances and, sometimes, even food and drink samples are all offered with good grace and without charge.

When it rains

Being the northernmost capital city in the world, and surrounded by the rain-bringing Gulf Stream, poor weather in Reykjavik is a common occurrence, and hardly changes the tourist itinerary. Much of what there is to see is equally fun to view with precipitation as with sun. With so much of interest in the city, rain often gives visitors a chance to peruse the art galleries and museums they would normally pass by. The Reykjavik Welcome Card includes entry to 14 cultural institutions. Shopping, too, becomes a pleasure when there is enough time to peruse the woollen clothing and photography books available only in Iceland. Then there are the things that the locals do themselves when the weather is unfriendly. On rainy days, Reykjavikers crowd into coffee houses, linger longer, and are often more chatty – even to visitors. There doesn't seem to be any rush and time slips away delightfully.

Spas and hot tubs are well patronised, and the outdoor thermal pools have even more attendees during rain than in sun. After all, you can't get any wetter! It might even be possible to get into a serious discussion with an Icelander, sitting in a very pleasantly warm outdoor hot pot while the rain pours. If excess energy is an issue, the excellent gym at Laugardalur is not only state of the art, but also a great place to be seen, and the hedonistic saunas, steam baths and showers of the adjoining Laugar Spa make all that hard work worth it.

The major museums are essentials, rain or shine, but some of the less-frequented galleries are also worth a look, especially when it's wet outside. The centrally located Ljósmyndasafn Reykjavikur (Reykjavik Museum of Photography) holds changing exhibitions and often shows images with Icelandic themes (see page 75). Further away but also very intriguing is the Ásmundarsafn (see page 96), the sculpture collection of Ásmundur Sveinsson, a favourite son of the country. Although there are outdoor pieces, the indoor ones are not only more indicative of the maker's style, but show off the extraordinary artist-designed residence.

As rain falls, heading into the shops of central Reykjavik is one way to pass the time. Up and down Laugavegur are unusual stores, while Skólavörðustígur is known for its craft items. Kringlan Mall, further away but completely undercover, is large enough to occupy a tourist in poor weather for a good afternoon at least (see page 100).

◗ Downtown cafés like Babalú (see page 82) are favourite haunts on rainy days

On arrival

TIME DIFFERENCE
Reykjavik is on Greenwich Mean Time (GMT) all year round.

ARRIVING
By air
Visitors flying into Iceland arrive at **Keflavík International Airport**
(W www.keflavikairport.com), which is located in the small town
of Keflavík, approximately 50 km (31 miles) west of Reykjavik's
city centre. Reykjavik does have its own airport close to the city
centre, but it only handles domestic services run by **Air Iceland**
(W www.airiceland.is) and flights to Greenland and the Faeroe Islands.
Keflavík airport is extremely modern, offering a wide range of services
to passengers. A post office, currency exchange, restaurants and
duty-free sales (for both arriving and departing passengers) are
available at the terminal, which was re-designed in 2008.

If you have not booked a transfer from the airport as part of
a package, the easiest and cheapest way to get to Reykjavik city
centre is by bus. The **Flybus** service (W www.flybus.is) is linked to
flight arrival and departure times and takes 45–50 minutes to get
from the airport to the main BSÍ Coach Terminal in town. Most
hotels and many guesthouses are on the itinerary and bus drivers
will stop at individual hotels if informed in advance. Adult fares
are approximately 1,700Kr. one way or 3,000Kr. return; children
aged 12–15 are half price and those under 11 travel free. Tickets are
available online, inside the arrivals hall of the terminal or at the
machine located next the exit.

Taxis are also available, although far more expensive than the
Flybus. The average fare to the centre of town is around 9,000Kr.

For more information, see Ⓦ www.airporttaxi.is.

If you're planning to hire a car (see page 66), you'll find the offices of most local car hire firms in the arrivals area. It's usually more convenient to hire a car at the airport than in town.

By water

Although most visitors choose to arrive by air, there is a regular scheduled passenger and car ferry service from Denmark to the port at Seyðisfjörður in eastern Iceland, operated by **Smyril Lines** (Ⓦ www.smyril-line.com). This somewhat convoluted journey takes three days and goes via the Faeroe Islands. There is no ferry service direct from the UK.

🔽 *An Icelandair plane in the snow at Keflavík International Airport*

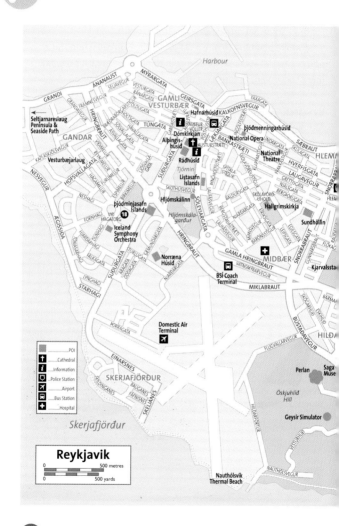

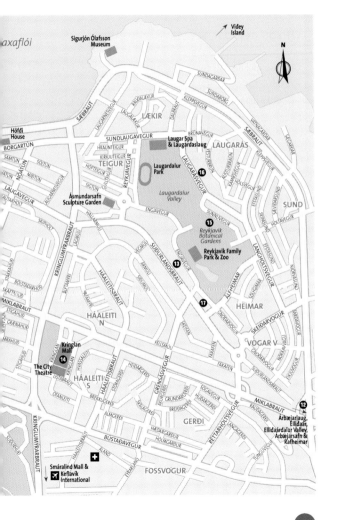

IF YOU GET LOST, TRY ...

Excuse me, do you speak English?
Afsakið, talar þú ensku?
Afsahkith, talahr thoo ensku?

How do I get to ...?
Hvernig kemst ég til ...?
Kvernikh kemst yehkh til ...?

Can you show me on my map?
Getur þú sýnt mér á kortinu?
Gehter thoo seent myehr ow kortinu?

From the port there are bus services to almost everywhere in Iceland, and the trip to Reykjavik, crossing the country from east to west, will take most of the day. For information on bus services outside the capital, visit Ⓦ www.nat.is

If travelling with a vehicle, to get to the capital the quickest way possible, take route 93 west to Egilsstaðir, then turn on to Iceland's ring road, route 1. It really doesn't matter much whether you head north or south – both directions take a long time (and each leads through incredible scenery) and eventually arrive in Reykjavik.

Cruise ships that ply the Arctic and have Iceland as one of their ports of call will arrive in Reykjavik. Some ships dock at the Old Harbour, minutes away from the city centre; others arrive at the larger Sundahöfn Harbour.

FINDING YOUR FEET

Central Reykjavik is very small and can be traversed on foot in half a day. Most things of tourist interest are within this area. However, the city officially covers 275 sq km (900 sq ft), of which only 45 sq km (150 sq ft) are densely populated, and this can be a lot bigger than it first seems. What looks on the map to be very close might take longer to reach than expected. This guide provides public transport options for destinations outside the central areas which cannot easily be reached on foot.

Note that areas within the postcode area 101 are located in the inner city centre, whereas other postcodes, such as 107 and 108, refer to areas which are slightly further afield and may require a bus ride or car journey.

Security wise, Reykjavik is probably one of the safest cities in Europe. Crime is rare and late-night walking in the tourist areas fine. Good sense is always advisable, but no special surveillance is necessary.

ORIENTATION

Reykjavik is on a peninsula jutting westward into the ocean. The suburban areas of Elliðaár and Laugardalur are to the east, and the city centre is to the west, nestling against the bayside harbour to the north. Just to the west of the centre and resting along the seaside is a residential area, and directly south of the city's heart is the domestic airport. On its east side is the recreational area of Öskjuhlíð, site of the Pearl and Nauthólsvík Beach.

Laugavegur is the street of most interest to the visitor and it runs east–northwest, beginning almost as far east as Laugardalur Valley. The interesting part of the street only starts, however, when it reaches Hlemmur, the site of one of Reykjavik's two main bus stations, when it begins to run parallel to the shoreline. To the

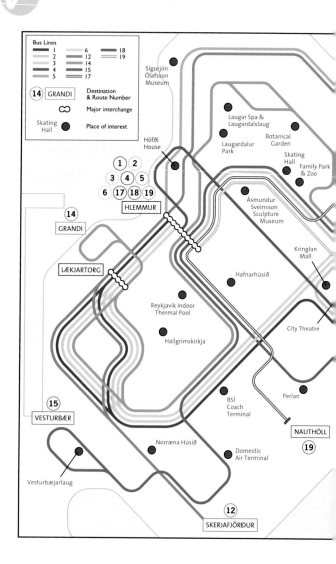

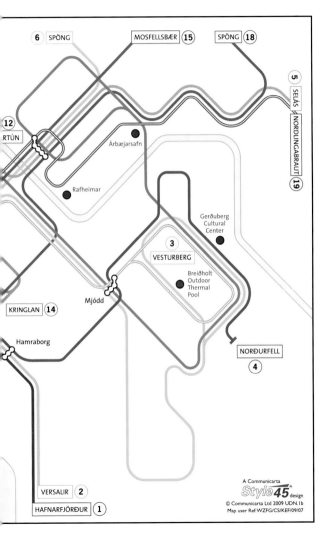

6 SPÖNG

MOSFELLSBÆR 15

SPÖNG 18

5 SELÁS

NORÐLINGABRAUT 19

12

RTÚN

Árbæjarsafn

Rafheimar

Gerðuberg
Cultural
Center

3

VESTURBERG

Breiðholt
Outdoor
Thermal
Pool

KRINGLAN 14

Mjódd

Hamraborg

NORÐURFELL

4

A Communicarta
Style 45 design
© Communicarta Ltd 2009 UDN.1b
Map user Ref:WZFG/CS/KEF/09/07

VERSALIR 2

HAFNARFJÖRÐUR 1

south and up the hill the dramatic Hallgrímskirkja, Reykjavik's most visible landmark, comes into view. Continuing on Laugavegur, the street then narrows and heads downhill where the name changes briefly to Bankastræti and then Austurstræti.

Just to the south of Austurstræti is Austurvollur Square. Straight ahead is the open area of Ingólfstorg Square where much of Reykjavik's festival life takes place, and on the opposite side of which is the main Reykjavik tourist office. To the north is the Old Harbour.

Turning south from the square will get you to the Ráðhúsið (City Hall) and Tjörnin (City Pond), which are always lovely places to visit. Just past the pond's west bank, and slightly to the south, is Þjóðminjasafn Íslands (National Museum of Iceland).

GETTING AROUND

Public transport in and around the capital consists of bus routes operated by **Straetó** (ⓦ www.bus.is). The main terminals are at Lækjartorg in the heart of the city and at Hlemmur, just to the east but still fairly central. 29 bus routes cover the whole city area as well as the neighbouring communities and usually run from 06.30 or 07.00 to 00.00 (except on Sundays and holidays, when they start between 11.30 and noon). An adult single fare is 280Kr. (100Kr. for children) and a block of 11 tickets costs 2,500Kr. It is best to purchase tickets in advance from major bus stops and from the Kringlan Mall, as no change can be given on the bus.

The Reykjavik Welcome Card includes unlimited use of Strætó buses for the duration of the card, as well as entry to most of the city's museums and all of its thermal pools, and is available for a 24-, 48- or 72-hour period. The card can be purchased from Tourist Information Centres, Strætó central bus stations, the BSÍ Coach Terminal and at a number of attractions and other outlets in the

ICELANDIC LETTERS

The Icelandic language has remained virtually unchanged since the time of settlement. It is most closely related to Faroese and, to some extent, Norwegian, although the grammar is much more complex. This guide uses Icelandic spelling for all words (except the name 'Reykjavik', which is spelled with an í in Icelandic). Icelandic letters are the same as those in English, with accents available on all vowels (á, é, í, ó, ú, and ý), as well as æ and ö. When speaking, the emphasis is almost always on the first syllable. Two ancient letters can sometimes create confusion among visitors:

Þ/þ or "thorn" is a soft 'th' sound, as in *think*.

Ð/ð or "eth" is a hard 'th' sound, as in *there*.

city. The cost at the time of writing is 1,400Kr. for 24 hours, 1,900Kr. for 48 hours and 2,400Kr. for 72 hours.

Taxis operate throughout the city. Though comparatively expensive, they are quick and efficient and arrive on time. All the official vehicles have meters and rates are standardised. As an example, a five- to ten-minute journey from the centre to the domestic airport will cost around 1,000Kr. Tipping is not necessary.

Taxi companies in the city include:

Borgarbílastöðin ☏ 552 2440

BSR taxis ☏ 561 0000

Hreyfill-Bæjarleiðir ☏ 588 5522

CAR HIRE

After a day or two in the city, the desire to explore the country will become pretty powerful. If excursions or day tours are not the answer, the possibilities for car hire are excellent. Iceland has several car rental companies, as well as wonderful countryside that begs to be seen. Most of the main roads are good to adequate.

A warning, however, that some of the routes that are mapped are 'F' or mountain (highland) roads. Four-wheel-drive vehicles are an absolute must for these thoroughfares, which are only open during summer, and sometimes even they are not powerful enough to deal with the conditions. Prices for rental, additional insurance and the high cost of extra petrol consumption make this option very costly although feasible. For a short break in Reykjavik, however, there are enough graded and partially graded roads to make driving, even in a conventional car, enough of an adventure.

Prices vary slightly between the companies, but generally a small economy car, collected and dropped off at Keflavík airport, with unlimited mileage and basic insurance, will cost around 22,000Kr. per day in the summer. Better deals can probably be made if booked in advance, and often the best prices are those included in a pre-booked package.

There are more than a dozen companies that rent out cars in and around Reykjavik, but the major ones are:

Avis ⊕ 591 4000 ⓦ www.avis.is
Budget ⊕ 562 6060 ⓦ www.budget.is
Europcar ⊕ 565 3800 ⓦ www.europcar.is
Hertz ⊕ 522 4400 ⓦ www.hertz.is

⊙ *The Pearl (see page 93) offers great views over the city*

 THE CITY OF
Reykjavik

Inner city & the harbour

Although Reykjavik sprawls over quite a large region, the inner city, where most things of tourist interest lie, is very small. At a sprint, the area can be covered in a couple of hours. Nevertheless, there is much to see. Several museums and art galleries are located centrally, as well as boutique and souvenir shopping. The city's history is visible here together with the distinctive brightly coloured corrugated iron houses that are identified with Reykjavik. Parks and sculptures punctuate the area.

The inner city, 101 Reykjavik, and the Old Harbour are where things are happening, and restaurants, coffee houses and clubs huddle here in a mass. These venues are often next door to each other, and a good

AN INNER-CITY WALK – PART 1

Begin at Lækjartorg, the true city centre and one of the bus station terminals, and walk towards the Tjörnin (City Pond). Cross the bridge towards Ráðhúsið (the City Hall), stopping to look at the relief map of Iceland for general orientation. Pass by, or if there's time, even step in to the Dómkirkjan (Cathedral) and Alþingishúsið (Parliament House), on the way to Aðalstræti. This area is very old; Aðalstræti 10, which now contains the popular design store Kraum and is next door to the Tourist Information Centre, is one of the city's original houses. Continue through the Grófin area, past the bright yellow Kaffi Reykjavik, to the picturesque harbour. Filled with brightly coloured fishing boats, this area is a delight to visit. Heading east, return to Lækjartorg.

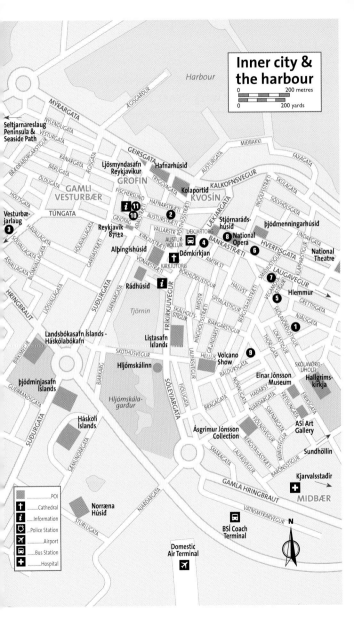

AN INNER-CITY WALK – PART 2

Walk southeast from Lakjartorg along Bankastræti. Head up the hill and begin window shopping, perhaps stopping at one of the cafés for a break. Follow the street until it comes to Hlemmur, the other bus terminal. Head south on Rauðarárstígur until reaching the Kjarvalsstaðir art museum. After the visit, meander westwards, crossing the larger street of Snorrabraut up the hill to Hallgrímskirja church. A look at the interior is a must and, on a clear day, so is a trip up to the tower to see the view. Head back into the centre via Skólavörðustígur and its fine arts and crafts shops, returning to Bankastræti.

pub crawl that lasts all night, and well into the morning, may not require anything more than walking – or staggering – down the street. Buses and taxis zigzag in and out of the pedestrian zones, but are not really needed except to go to outer Reykjavik or further afield.

SIGHTS & ATTRACTIONS

Aðalstræti

In the early days of Reykjavik this was the original, and for a while, only, street in the city. Full of Icelandic charm missing in other more modernised parts of the city, this is a good spot to watch kids skateboarding in the nearby Ingólfstorg Square, have a glass of wine, or take in a museum. The city's **Tourist Information Centre** is here (📍 Aðalstræti 2, 101 📞 590 1500 🌐 www.visitreykjavik.is 🚌 Bus: 1, 3, 6, 11, 12, 13, 14).

⬥ The iconic Hallgrímskirkja took nearly 40 years to construct

Alþingishúsið (Parliament)

Not much to look at, but historically very important, this grey basalt building is the national seat of Parliament. Originally at Þingvellir since AD 930, the body was disbanded when the Danish took power. In 1881, seven years after being granted a constitution, the building was constructed. In 1944, Iceland became an independent nation. ❶ Kirkjustræti, 101 ☎ 563 0500 ❿ www.althingi.is ◷ Garden: 24 hrs; free Parliament tours by arrangement ❷ Bus: 1, 3, 6, 11, 12, 13, 14

Hallgrímskirkja (Hallgrímur's Church)

The tallest and certainly most distinctive building in Reykjavik, Hallgrímskirkja resembles a rocket ship. Begun in 1949 but finished only in 1986, the interior is surprisingly peaceful considering the radical exterior. For a small fee, it's possible to ascend the 75 m (250 ft) tower for a spectacular view of the city. ❶ Skólavörðuholti, 101 ☎ 510 1000 ❿ www.hallgrimskirkja.is ◷ 09.00–17.00 ❷ Bus: 14, 15, 18, 19

Lækjartorg Square

Not so much an attraction but rather a point of orientation, this square is at the geographic, if not spiritual, heart of the central city. One of the city's bus terminals is here. At the top of the grassy hill is a statue of Ingólfur Arnarson, the Norwegian Viking credited with being the city's first settler (see page 14). ❷ Bus: 1, 3, 6, 11, 12, 13, 14

Laugavegur–Bankastræti–Skólavörðustígur

101 Reykjavik's main shopping streets run into each other. Laugavegur is the longest, running east–northwest, and is full of quirky and high-fashion shops. At its northwestern end it turns into Bankastræti,

◉ *Brightly coloured fishing boats add to the ambience of the harbour*

which leads to the centre of the city. At an angle to Laugavegur, leading literally up to Hallgrímskirkja, is Skólavörðustígur, a street which is developing a reputation as the art (shop and gallery) avenue. Bus: 1, 3, 6, 11, 12, 13, 14

The Old Harbour

Commercially replaced by the central harbour around Sæbraut, the Old Harbour has been left for tourist seagoing excursions and for its charm. Tiny fishing boats are moored here, as well as what's left of the old whaling fleet. Whale- and puffin-watching trips leave from here in the season (see page 41). ⓝ Bus: 1, 3, 6, 11, 12, 13, 14

Ráðhúsið (City Hall)

This modern building, constructed in 1992, successfully blends its indoor and outdoor aspects while sitting atop of the City Pond. Open to the public, it's worth entering to see the huge relief map of Iceland as well as whatever exhibition may be on show. A coffee bar and public toilets add to its appeal. ⓐ Tjarnargata, 101 ⓣ 411 1000 ⓒ 08.30–19.00 Mon–Fri, 10.00–18.00 Sat & Sun, mid-May–mid-Sept; 10.30–18.00 Mon–Fri, 12.00–18.00 Sat & Sun, mid-Sept–mid-May ⓝ Bus: 1, 3, 6, 11, 12, 13, 14

The Seaside Path

Reykjavik has an unbeatable walking and cycling path that envelops the city from the harbour, around the Seltjarnarnes Peninsula, and all the way to the Pearl. It's a great way to take in the scope of the city on a sunny morning or, in winter, after a fresh snowfall, though it can get a little windy in parts. Bring your togs and stop for a swim along the way in the Seltjarnarneslaug or Vesturbæjarlaug swimming pools. ⓝ Bus: 1, 3, 6, 11, 12, 13, 14

Tjörnin (City Pond)

Reykjavik's city 'pond' is more of a lake, a delightful rural aspect in the midst of the urban environment. Strolling along the banks offers excellent views of the city to the east, while a shooting fountain casts a rainbow over the scene on sunny days. Waterfowl linger on the shore hoping for handouts. Ⓝ Bus: 1, 3, 6, 11, 12, 13, 14

CULTURE

Hafnarhúsið (Reykjavik Art Museum)

The Art Museum's headquarters are creatively housed in an old warehouse in the port. Six halls contain the permanent collection, including works by Icelandic pop artist Erró, and temporary exhibitions of both Icelandic and foreign artists. Entry is free. Ⓐ Tryggvagata 17, 101 Ⓣ 590 1200 Ⓦ www.artmuseum.is. Ⓛ 10.00–17.00 Fri–Wed, 10.00–22.00 Thur Ⓝ Bus: 1, 3, 6, 11, 12, 13, 14

Listasafn Íslands (National Gallery of Iceland)

Foreign and domestic painters are well represented here in a gallery that was founded in 1884. Entry is free and a shop and restaurant are on-site. Ⓐ Fríkirkjuvegur 7, 101 Ⓣ 515 9600 Ⓦ www.listasafn.is Ⓛ 11.00–17.00 Tues–Sun Ⓝ Bus: 1, 3, 6, 11, 12, 13, 14

Ljósmyndasafn Reykjavikur (Reykjavik Museum of Photography)

Sharing premises with the City Library, this free museum has several exhibitions annually, both independently and in conjunction with other organisations. Ⓐ Grófarhús (6th floor), Tryggvagata 15, 101 Ⓣ 411 6390 Ⓦ www.ljosmyndasafnreykjavikur.is Ⓛ 12.00–19.00 Mon–Fri, 13.00–17.00 Sat & Sun Ⓝ Bus: 1, 3, 6, 11, 12, 13, 14

⬣ Iceland's history is impressively displayed at the National Museum

Reykjavik 871±2 The Settlement Exhibition

Reykjavik's most modern heritage museum is built on the ruins of an ancient Viking longhouse, discovered here in 2001. The multimedia exhibition explores Iceland's Viking history via the city's oldest ruins. A wonderful design gift shop is attached. ⓐ Aðalstræti 16, 101 ⓣ 411 6370 ⓦ www.reykjavik871.is ⓛ 10.00–17.00 ⓝ Bus: 1, 3, 6, 11, 12, 13, 14

Þjóðmenningarhúsið (The Culture House)

The jewel in this collection is the permanent display of medieval manuscripts. The well-presented vellum texts are the oldest accounts remaining of Iceland's greatest literary works, the Sagas. The other permanent and changing exhibitions have national relevance, and are usually interesting, too. Admission is free on Wednesdays. ⓐ Hverfisgata 15, 101 ⓣ 545 1400 ⓦ www.thjodmenning.is ⓛ 11.00–17.00 ⓝ Bus: 1, 3, 6, 12, 14, 15

Þjóðminjasafn Íslands (National Museum of Iceland)

Completely renovated in late 2004, this state-of-the-art museum depicts the 1,200 years of Iceland's social and cultural history. The displays are extremely well presented using the latest exhibition technology. A branch of the coffee house Kaffitár helps give the visitor enough stamina to get through the large exhibitions, and the gift shop here is possibly the best place to buy interesting souvenirs in the country. Admission is free on Wednesdays and there are guided tours in English daily at 11.00 between June and mid-September, and on Saturdays at 14.00 during the rest of the year. ⓐ Suðurgata 41, 107 ⓣ 530 2200 ⓦ www.natmus.is ⓛ 10.00–17.00 Tues–Sun, May–mid-Sept; 11.00–17.00 Tues–Sun, mid-Sept–Apr ⓝ Bus: 1, 12, 14, 15

RETAIL THERAPY

Most of 101 Reykjavik is laden with boutiques, stores, bars and restaurants, although the primary shopping streets are Laugavegur, Skólavörðustígur, Bankastræti and Austurstræti.

Street markets are not really a feature in the city – the outdoor fruit and vegetable stalls are often health-food stores advertising their slightly more expensive produce. However, the Kolaportið flea market is fun with its collection of strange second-hand items and even weirder Icelandic food items.

12 Tonar In its well-known little yellow house down the street from the church, this independent music store has the best collection of Icelandic jazz, classical, folk and rock music you'll find. You can listen to tunes before you buy. ⓐ Skólavörðustígur 15, 101 ☎ 511 5656 ⓦ www.12tonar.is 🕐 10.00–18.00 Mon–Fri, 10.00–14.00 Sat; also open 13.00–17.00 Sun in summer

66° North Iceland's home-grown, all-weather clothing company has as its catchphrase 'there is no bad weather – just the wrong clothing'. The expensive but well-made clothes suit the Icelandic climate perfectly. ⓐ Bankastræti 5, 101 ☎ 517 6020 ⓦ www.66north.is 🕐 10.00–18.00 Mon–Fri, 11.00–16.00 Sat, 11.00–17.00 Sun

Ásta Creative Clothes A fixture among Iceland's surprisingly prolific fashion designers, Ásta's third-floor shop on Reykjavik's main shopping street carries interesting dresses, hats and leggings that incorporate traditional Icelandic wool with a modern, feminine twist. Not cheap, but a one-of-a-kind souvenir. ⓐ Laugavegur 15, 101 ☎ 561 1949 ⓦ www.astaclothes.is 🕐 11.00–18.00 Mon–Fri, 11.00–16.00 Sat

◯ *In a building next to the harbour, Kolaportið is the city's flea market*

Blue Lagoon Spa Shop The famous hot spring resort has a conveniently located shop in town. The cosmetics and skin-care products are made from a combination of minerals, silica and algae and are supposed to be great for skin (but awful for hair!). ⓐ Laugavegur 15, 101 ⓣ 420 8849 ⓦ www.bluelagoon.com ⓛ 10.00–18.00 Mon–Fri, 10.00–16.00 Sat, 13.00–17.00 Sun, summer; 10.00–18.00 Mon–Fri, 11.00–16.00 Sat, winter

Hans Petersen This good general camera supply shop is well located in the centre of town. Hans Petersen is the main Kodak dealer in Iceland. ⓐ Bankastræti 4, 101 ⓣ 412 1810 ⓦ www.hanspetersen.is ⓛ 10.00–18.00 Mon–Fri, 11.00–16.00 Sat

IDA English is almost as widely spoken as Icelandic here, and this modern bookshop caters to Iceland's second language extremely well. There is a large range of newspapers, postcards, gift-wrapping supplies – and even books. ⓐ Lækjargata 2A ⓣ 511 5001 ⓦ www.ida.is ⓛ 09.00–22.00

Kisan A concept shop specialising in French imports such as Bon Point baby clothes and Sonia Rykiel. Its windows are always fun to check out, and its ever whimsical stock inside is even better. ⓐ Laugavegur 7, 101 ⓣ 561 6262 ⓦ www.kisan.is ⓛ 10.30–18.00 Mon–Thur, 10.30–19.30 Fri, 10.30–18.00 Sat

Kolaportið Reykjavik's famous harbourside flea market is located in an old port building, entered from Tryggavagata street. It's famous for offbeat items, ranging from old rock memorabilia to vintage clothing and antique books. The food section is particularly well known, selling uniquely Icelandic items such as *harðfiskur* (dried

strips of fish eaten like crisps) and *hákarl* (rotten shark meat).
🅐 Tryggvagötu 19, 101 ☎ 562 5030 🅦 www.kolaportid.is
🕐 11.00–17.00 Sat & Sun

Ostabúðin Probably Reykjavik's premier delicatessen and a wonderful
place to view, as well as to buy. Icelandic and foreign cheeses
are especially well represented. Light lunches are also served.
🅐 Skólavörðustígur 8, 101 ☎ 562 2772 🅦 www.ostabudin.is
🕐 11.00–18.00 Mon–Thur, 11.00–18.30 Fri, 11.00–16.00 Sat

Vínbúð The government-run off-licence has several locations
throughout the city, although this one is the most centrally
located. Stop here for a somewhat cheaper beer or bottle of wine
and, like the Icelanders, start the drinking before going to the pub.
🅐 Austurstræti 10A, 101 ☎ 562 6511 🅦 www.vinbud.is 🕐 11.00–18.00
Mon–Thur, 11.00–19.00 Fri, 11.00–18.00 Sat

TAKING A DIP

Enjoying thermal pools is not just a leisure activity – it's more
an Icelandic way of life. The word *laug*, which appears regularly,
including in the name of the city's premier shopping street,
Laugavegur, means 'pool'. Most Reykjavikers indulge in a regular
swim, and it's often the spot for some heated discussion, so to speak.

Sundhöllin A neoclassical-style pool built in 1940, this is Reykjavik's
only thermal pool that's under cover. 🅐 Barónsstígur 45, 101
☎ 411 5350 🕐 06.30–21.30 Mon–Fri, 08.00–19.00 Sat & Sun
🅝 Bus: 14, 15, 18, 19

Vesturbæjarlaug A pool that is conveniently within walking distance of pretty much anywhere in the city centre. ⓐ Hofsvallagata, 107 ⓣ 551 5004 ⓛ 06.30–22.00 Mon–Fri, 08.00–20.00 Sat & Sun ⓝ Bus: 15, 11

TAKING A BREAK

Babalú £ ❶ An upstairs café with antique furniture, great coffee, background music and a lovely deck for sunny days. ⓐ Skólavörðustígur 22A, 101 ⓣ 555 8845 ⓛ 11.00–23.00

Café Paris £ ❷ Prominently placed in the centre of town, this is a great spot to order a jug of coffee and watch the world go by. Meals are served but service is generally slow. ⓐ Austurstræti 14, 101 ⓣ 551 1020 ⓦ www.cafeparis.is ⓛ 09.00–01.00 Sun–Thur, 08.00–04.00 Fri & Sat

Ísbúð Vesturbæjar £ ❸ Reykjavik's most famous ice cream shop – and there are many ice cream shops – is conveniently located down the street from Vesturbæjarlaug, the pool in the west part of town. Packed late every night, Ísbúð's vanilla comes in two varieties: milky or creamy. Locals go for milky. ⓐ Hagamelur 67, 107 ⓣ 552 3330 ⓛ 13.00–23.30 Mon–Fri, 12.00–23.30 Sat & Sun ⓝ Bus: 15, 11

Kaffitár £ ❹ One of the more popular places to hang out and have a break, this colourful coffee house has a range of different coffee beans from around the world. There are also outlets in the National Museum and in Kringlan Mall. ⓐ Bankastræti 8, 101 ⓣ 511 4540 ⓦ www.kaffitar.is ⓛ 07.30–18.00 Mon–Sat, 10.00–17.00 Sun

Mokka £ ❺ The oldest café in Reykjavik is a fantastic, atmospheric little place to stop in on a rainy day for one of the famous hot chocolates and a waffle with whipped cream. ⓐ Skólavörðustígur 3A, 101 ❶ 552 1174 ⓦ www.mokka.is ❶ 09.00–18.30

AFTER DARK

RESTAURANTS

Café Sólon £ ❻ A true Reykjavik coffee house and restaurant, this is a place where you can spend hours eating and chatting with friends or just sipping a drink and people-watching. ⓐ Bankastræti 7A, 101 ❶ 562 3232 ⓦ www.solon.is ❶ 11.00–00.00 Mon–Wed, 11.00–01.00 Thur–Sat, 12.00–00.00 Sun (kitchen closes 22.00)

Vegamot £ ❼ Casual but well-attended combo venue; the food is international and the décor Mediterranean. Lots of regulars come here, and it's possible to hang out until the place turns into somewhere a bit more lively. ⓐ Vegamótastígur 4, 101 ❶ 511 3040 ⓦ www.vegamot.is ❶ 11.00–01.00 Mon–Thur, 11.00–05.00 Fri & Sat, 12.00–01.00 Sun (kitchen closes 22.00 Sun–Thur, 23.30 Fri & Sat)

b5 £–££ ❽ A perfect place for a coffee, dessert, three-course dinner or a cocktail, b5 is what so many of the restaurants in Reykjavik try to be but don't quite manage – hip, sleek and always inviting. ⓐ Bankastræti 5, 101 ❶ 552 9600 ⓦ www.b5.is ❶ 11.00–22.00

Þrír Frakkar ££ ❾ A small restaurant slightly off the beaten track, but still in the centre, where diners nevertheless have a sense of being in on a well-guarded secret. With traditional dishes prepared in the old-fashioned way, offerings on the menu include catfish, puffin

⬣ *While away a few hours chatting and people-watching at a coffee house*

and whale. ❸ Baldursgata 14, 101 ❶ 552 3939 Ⓦ www.3frakkar.com
🕒 11.30–14.30, 18.00–22.00 Mon–Fri, 18.00–23.00 Sat & Sun

Fish Market £££ ❿ Fish Market has been a hit with locals and tourists
alike since it opened in one of Reykjavik's oldest buildings in 2007,
and now rivals Sjávarkjallarinn as the capital's best seafood eatery.
The chef sources many ingredients directly from local farmers and
fishermen, creating traditional dishes with a modern twist, attractively
presented. ❸ Aðalstræti 12, 101 ❶ 578 8877 Ⓦ www.fishmarket.is
🕒 11.30–14.00, 18.00–23.30 Mon–Fri, 18.00–23.30 Sat & Sun

Sjávarkjallarinn £££ ⓫ The 'Seafood Cellar' is a fine restaurant and
arguably the best in town. If you can get past its bland name and
location in the basement of the city's main tourist office, you will
not be disappointed by this fusion splurge that will challenge and
delight the international foodie palette. Quite pricey, but a real
treat by any big city standards. ❸ Aðalstræti 2, 101 ❶ 511 1212
Ⓦ www.sjavarkjallarinn.is 🕒 18.00–22.30 Sun–Thur, 18.00–23.30
Fri & Sat

BARS & CLUBS

There are a tremendous number of places to hang out until the
wee hours. The venues are very fluid, however, with places going in
and out of business quickly, and even more fleeting is their moment
of fashion. Check with the monthly listings guides (see page 37)
for updates.

At weekends, when the parties happen, nothing much occurs
till midnight, and then the action goes on until about 05.00
or 06.00.

Barbara An informal but energetic bar and club, located on the second and third floors of a former Reykjavik home. It welcomes both gay and straight clubbers and the music style differs from night to night. 🅐 Laugavegur 22 🕿 694 1774 🕐 21.00–05.00 Fri & Sat

Hemmi og Valdi Laid-back café by day and heaving nightclub by night, Nýlenduvöruverslun Hemma&Valda (Hemmi og Valdi for short) is renowned for the huge jugs of beer on offer. After midnight at weekends, the place is packed to bursting with a young, fun crowd. 🅐 Laugavegur 21 🕿 551 6464 🅦 www.verzlun.com 🕐 10.00–01.00 Sun–Thur, 10.00–03.00 Fri & Sat.

Kaffibarinn A London underground sign welcomes visitors to this little bar up the hill from Laugavegur. It can get a bit rowdy late at night. 🅐 Bergstadastræti 1, 101 🕿 551 1588 🕐 15.00–01.00 Sun–Thur, 15.00–05.00 Fri & Sat

Óliver An enduringly trendy bistro-club in Reykjavik. The restaurant does have an unofficial dress code, the locals can be a bit arrogant, and you have to wait in a long line if you arrive after 23.00. Still, it is a place to be seen. 🅐 Laugavegur 20A, 101 🕿 552 2300 🅦 www.cafeoliver.is 🕐 11.45 – 01.00 Mon–Thur, 11.45 – 04.30 Fri, 15.00–04.30 Sat, 15.00–01.00 Sun (kitchen closes 22.00)

Prikið Despite catering to a younger crowd, this bar is one of Reykjavik's oldest. Located in the heart of things on Bankastræti. Food and coffee are also served. 🅐 Bankastræti 12, 101 🕿 551 2866 🅦 www.prikid.is 🕐 08.00–01.00 Mon–Thur, 08.00–05.30 Fri, 12.00–05.30 Sat, 12.00–01.00 Sun

Vínbarinn A little off the normal pub-crawl route both for its location behind Parliament and its subdued atmosphere, this wine bar has big, bright windows and an excellent wine selection with staff who know what they're talking about. ⓐ Kirkjutorg 4, 101 ⓣ 552 4120 ⓛ 16.00–01.00 Mon–Thur, 16.00–03.00 Fri & Sat

CINEMAS & THEATRES

National Theatre Iceland's National Theatre company performs international and national plays, while also premiering between ten and fourteen original pieces every year. The architecture of the rather dour but impressive building is based on basalt columns taken from Iceland's volcanic scenery. ⓐ Hverfisgata 19, 101 ⓣ 551 1200 ⓦ www.leikhusid.is

Regnboginn Cinema A multi-screen cinema showing a mix of new releases and art-house films. It's also the venue for various film festivals; check monthly listings guides to find out what's on. ⓐ Hverfisgata 54, 101 ⓣ 551 9000

Beyond the centre

Beyond the compact centre where one can find most of Reykjavik's sights, are the sprawling suburbs. At this point the capital begins to resemble an American city, rather than a European one, with fairly large distances between attractions and just a few too many miles to walk. Here public transport comes into its own, with the bus service making the outer city almost as accessible as the inner. See the map on page 58 for the location of sights, cafés and restaurants in this section.

The country reverts to its natural state quite quickly, and even within the official city limits scenery begins to overwhelm the residential development. The chain of parks that begins with Tjörnin, the pond surrounding the City Hall, begin to get closer to each other until they come together at the Elliðaár, the city's fishable salmon river. At the edges, it's hard to tell where Reykjavik ends and the countryside begins.

There are three areas of particular interest in the outer city: Laugardalur Valley, Öskjuhlíð Hill and Elliðaárdalur Valley.

SIGHTS & ATTRACTIONS

LAUGARDALUR VALLEY

The story goes that the explorers who first spotted the site of the future capital called the area 'Reykja-vík', or 'smoky bay'. What they assumed was smoke rising from fires was actually steam from the natural hot springs that are found here. Their existence is most likely the reason that the city's biggest thermal pool was built on this spot. Surrounding it is the nation's best sporting facility and a large sports stadium, home to the Icelandic football team, as well as to most of its athletic events. Also in the area is Ásmundarsafn Sculpture Garden, a branch of the Reykjavik Art Museum that features the work of Ásmundur Sveinsson, Reykjavik Family Park & Zoo and the Reykjavik Botanical Gardens. Ⓝ Bus: 2, 14, 15, 17, 19

Laugar Spa

Less affordable than Laugardalur Park (see below) but far more luxurious is the Laugar Spa centre. The gym is a huge state-of-the-art workout zone with hundreds of pieces of equipment designed to keep locals fit and healthy. Before and after the usual business day the gym is packed. Adjoining the gym is the hedonistic spa, a place designed to allow the visitor to wallow in water-based indulgences. There are several steam baths, a few with soothing lighting and subtle earth smells rising up through the mist. Some of the saunas seem to have shockingly high temperatures, which make the consequent cold showers (in the shape of waterfalls) particularly refreshing. All the usual treatments are on offer, such as mud packs and massages. There are professional medical practitioners on the staff, as well as beauticians, nutritionists, manicurists and a range of people whose aim is to make the participant feel and look well. A restaurant serving healthy food and, surprisingly, wine is hiding in the back within the spa, and it's possible to sit in a bathrobe among the candles and soft music and nibble away. Ⓐ Sundlaugavegur 30, 105 Ⓣ 553 0000 Ⓦ www.laugarspa.is Ⓛ 06.00–23.30 Mon–Fri, 08.00–22.00 Sat, 08.00–20.00 Sun Ⓝ Bus: 2, 14, 15, 17, 19

Laugardalur Park

This complex is where many of the city's inhabitants come to get fit and have fun. The grounds offer football fields, for both the popular Icelandic international team and the weekend player. There is also the large athletic stadium where people seriously train all year round. Other facilities include a tennis and badminton hall and a skating rink.

Probably the best thing for the visitor to do is to indulge in the geothermally heated waters. The Laugardalur outdoor area consists of two outdoor pools, one for serious laps and the other for splashing around. In the open-air are also eight hot pots, a whirlpool and a wading pool. Inside is another competition arena for the country's professionals as well as the nation's keener amateur swimmers. The entry fees are low enough, and the opening hours amenable enough, for almost everyone to have the money and the time to come here.

🕐 Hours vary; check with the tourist office Ⓝ Bus: 2, 14, 15, 17, 19

Reykjavik Botanical Gardens

Though open all year, these gardens are best in the summer. Featuring mostly Icelandic plants, with a few foreign species thrown in for variety, this assembly has been open since 1961. There are research projects underlying the leisure aspect – scientists are experimenting with how the flora adapts to the country's relatively harsh environment.

ⓐ Laugardalur Valley, 104 ☎ 411 8650 Ⓦ www.grasagardur.is
🕐 10.00–22.00 Apr–Sept; 10.00–17.00 Oct–Mar Ⓝ Bus: 2, 15, 17, 19

Reykjavik Family Park & Zoo

Comprising three sections, the Family Park, Zoo and Science World is an ideal place to take the kids. Open all year, there's always something going on to interest everyone.

The speciality of the Zoo is to show Icelandic animals (of which there are virtually no endemic species – most of these home-grown creatures are farm animals). There are some examples of non-native wildlife which have adapted to the climactic conditions, such as foxes and reindeer. Activities for children include riding on an Icelandic horse.

▶ *Swim, play or just sit in one of the pools at Laugar*

▲ *A hot pot is just the place to recover from shopping and sightseeing*

The Family Park has a playground and activities. There is a café and a grill, if summer visitors want to barbecue their own hot dogs. Science World opened in 2004 and is continually growing. Featuring a touching and feeling display, active participation in the exhibitions is encouraged. The emphasis is on science and new technologies. ❸ Hafrafell, Engjavegur, 104 ❶ 575 7800 ❿ www.husdyragardur.is ◷ 10.00–18.00 June–mid-Aug; 10.00–17.00 mid-Aug–May Ⓝ Bus: 2, 15, 17, 19

ÖSKJUHLÍÐ HILL

This area's most prominent landmark is the Pearl, visible from much of the city. Though the hill isn't that high, and it's easy enough to ascend the mound on foot, the elevation is just enough to grant great views over the rest of Reykjavik. The whole area surrounding the building is a park, with hiking and biking trails, picnic tables and even a beach.

Nauthólsvík Thermal Beach

Down the other side of the hill, past the airport and into the wooded area, are walking and jogging paths that lead to the sea. Here, along the sound, is a golden beach, filled with bathers on warm summer days. Built by importing sand and roping off and excluding the cold natural sea, the thermal beach was created by harnessing the city's hot-water runoff from the central heating systems. The beach has been awarded the Blue Flag Certificate, an assurance that the place is maintaining a high quality clean and safe environment. Other activities are on offer around the beach. You can rent rowing boats for up to seven people as well as kayaks from **Siglunes** (❶ 551 3177). Sailing tours are also on offer; check with the Tourist Information Centre for tour times and operators. Bikes go whizzing past and the more energetic jog by. Nearby is the new campus of Reykjavik University, so expect plenty of student life during term time.

Perlan (The Pearl)

This strange building looking like a glorified series of water tanks is, in fact, just that. Composed of six hot-water storage facilities used for heating the city, the architect covered the assembly with a glass dome, and created a major tourist attraction. Just under the dome is one of Reykjavik's best known (but very touristy) restaurants; you're better off heading to the café below for an ice cream or snack. Step outside on a clear day, and the 360° view of the city and its surroundings is wonderful. Hiking and biking trails loop around the forested area beneath the building.

⬤ *The unmistakeable form of the Pearl sits on top of Öskjuhlíð Hill*

Also within the building are occasional exhibits and a fountain that sporadically spurts up three floors. One of the six tanks has been emptied of water and filled with the Saga Museum (see page 98), a collection of wax figures recreating the old days of Iceland.

In the grounds is another spurting fountain imitating the activities of one of the country's most famous geysers, Strokkur. ❸ Öskjuhlíð, 105 ❶ 562 0200 ❷ From 10.00 (closing times vary) ❿ www.perlan.is ❷ Bus: 18

ELLIÐAÁRDALUR VALLEY

Some way to the east of the centre but still within the city limits is the green valley of Elliðaárdalur. There is a distinctly rural feeling here, helped by the salmon river running through the middle. Declared a municipal conservation area for its wildlife, it's a popular recreation spot. Within this region are Reykjavik's open-air museum, Árbærsafn, a thermal pool and the Reykjavik Energy Museum (see page 98). ❷ Bus: 12, 18, 19, 24

Salmon fishing

Salmon numbers have increased again after a recent decline due to disease. For those who cannot afford a licence, it's still pleasurable to walk around the banks. The fishing season runs from 21 June to 13 August and permits are available from the **Angling Club of Reykjavik** (❸ Háaleitisbraut 68, 108 ❶ 568 6050 ❿ www.svfr.is). UK travellers can email ❻ peter@aardvarkmcleod.com to arrange a permit in advance.

VIÐEY ISLAND

A great way to spend a sunny day is to take a ferry out to Viðey Island in the middle of Reykjavik's bay. Its prime attraction is the Imagine Peace Tower, created by Yoko Ono in memory of her late husband, former Beatle John Lennon. The tower is actually a wishing well from which a strong, tall tower of light emerges at certain times of the year. The light shines annually between 9 October (Lennon's birthday) and 8 December (the day of his death), as well as during the winter solstice, first week of spring, and other special occasions. You can also stroll or ride a (free) bike over the bumpy trails, see the resident horses and visit the ruins of the former village, whose last inhabitant left in 1943. There's a café on the island but little else in the way of facilities. ❶ 533 5055 ❿ www.videy.com Ⓝ Bus: 5, 12 to ferry port, then ferry (call for times)

CULTURE

Árbæjarsafn (Árbær Museum)

This town – recreated in the middle of Elliðaárdalur's fields – is the Reykjavik City Museum's collection of historic buildings. Most of the houses are from the city, brought here rather than torn down, to preserve urban Icelandic heritage. There are a few remnants from the farm that was once here, and they blend in well with the period. Residences of the rich (including one that used to be the British Embassy), as well as the poor, populate this little metropolis. Also in the grounds are examples of the endemic turf house, storage areas built half underground, with grass growing on the roof.

Guides in historic costumes explain a bit more about the social history of the period and there's a small petting farm with sheep and horses. ⓐ Kistuhylur, 110, Elliðaárdalur Valley ① 411 6300 ⓦ www.arbaejarsafn.is ⑤ 10.00–17.00 June–August; guided tours only 13.00 Mon, Wed & Fri, Sept–May ⓝ Bus: 19

Ásmundarsafn Sculpture Garden

Ásmundur Sveinsson was a very popular native sculptor who died in 1982. Inspired by his own country, with its wild scenery and folkloric elements, he created sculpture that sprang from his national feeling. Sometimes controversial, his work changed from massive statues in the 1930s to abstract constructions made just before his death.

Ásmundur designed his house-cum-studio in a radical fashion, with architectural elements taken from distant sources, such as the pyramids in Egypt. He combined these influences in an extraordinary building, which now serves as the Reykjavik Art Museum's 'wing' for his work. Outside are several large pieces, providing a sculpture garden. Within are the more delicate items, including working models in several media, as well as sketches and drawings. A surprisingly nice presentation, with good work, but in some ways the building is more interesting than the art. Admission is free. ⓐ Sigtún, 105 (across from Laugardalur) ① 553 2155 ⓦ www.artmuseum.is ⑤ 10.00–16.00 May–Sept; 13.00–16.00 Oct–Apr ⓝ Bus: 2, 15, 17, 19

⬥ *Ásmundur Sveinsson's home is as much an attraction as his works of art*

Kjarvalsstaðir (Reykjavik Art Museum)

The nationally beloved 20th-century landscape painter Jóhannes S. Kjarval is the museum's eponymous painter as well as one of its exhibitors. The modern gallery also displays other contemporary artists. The restaurant has fine views over the museum's lawns. Admission is free. ⓐ Flókagata, 105 (north of Öskjuhlíð Hill) ⓣ 517 1290 ⓦ www.artmuseum.is ⓛ 10.00–17.00 ⓝ Bus: 13

Rafheimar (Reykjavik Energy Museum)

In 1899 the city lit up for the first time, and since 1921 most of Reykjavik's electricity supply has come from the power station in the Elliðaárdalur Valley. In order to explain the workings to the public, the electricity company opened up a museum in 1990. When the broader-based Municipal Energy Authority was founded in 1999, the museum changed its name – and its content – to cover all the sorts of energy involved in powering up the modern city. Now encompassing the Municipal Water and Geothermal heating works, the Reykjavik Energy Museum goes into detail as to how the city creates its power.

Also on display are exhibits that include folk history and technical development as they pertain to energy. On the ground floor is the mostly school-visited PowerWorld, which explains a bit more about electricity. On occasions the power station is open to the public and tours are given. ⓐ Elliðaárdalur Valley ⓣ 516 6790 ⓦ www.or.is ⓛ 13.00–16.00 Mon–Fri, Sept–May; 13.00–16.00 Mon–Fri, 14.00–16.00 Sat, June–Aug ⓝ Bus: 12, 19, 24

Saga Museum

Located within one of the Pearl's now defunct hot-water storage tanks (see page 93), this museum tells of decisive events in Iceland's

◆ The history of Iceland is revealed at the Saga Museum

history, using waxwork-like silicone figures. To make everything as authentic as possible, accessories are all made in the traditional way. Even the clothing is hand dyed. The guide, however, is more modern – each visitor is handed an MP3 player on entry. ⓐ Öskjuhlíð, 105 ⓣ 511 1517 ⓦ www.sagamuseum.is ⓛ 10.00–18.00 Apr–Sept; 12.00–17.00 Oct–Mar ⓝ Bus: 18

RETAIL THERAPY

Búrið A delightful new cheese shop just off Laugavegur. The Scots-Icelandic owner stocks stilton and aged cheddar as well as Icelandic specials like black gouda and goat's milk brie. Perfect for that picnic in the park. ⓐ Nóatún 17, 105 ⓣ 551 8400 ⓦ www.burid.is ⓛ 11.00–19.00 Mon–Fri, 12.00–18.00 Sat ⓝ Bus: 1, 2, 3, 4, 5, 6, 17, 18, 19

Kringlan Mall Reykjavik's giant mall is located about 4 km (2½ miles) from the city centre, close to Öskjuhlíð Hill. The super-size shopping centre contains about 150 shops, restaurants and services, including many European chain stores as well as local Icelandic shops. The mall also has a bank, food court, multi-screen cinema and supermarket, so it's a handy place to head to on a rainy day or if you have children to keep entertained. ⓐ Kringlan 4–12, 103 ⓣ 517 9000 ⓦ www.kringlan.is ⓛ 10.00–18.30 Mon–Wed, 10.00–19.00 Thur & Fri, 10.00–18.00 Sat, 13.00–17.00 Sun ⓝ Bus: 1, 2, 3, 4, 6, 13, 14

Laugar Spa The 5-star spa also has a sports shop, if a spare bathing suit or a pair of gym shorts is needed. ⓐ Sundlaugavegur 30A, 104 ⓣ 553 0000 ⓦ www.laugarspa.is ⓛ 06.00–23.30 Mon–Fri, 08.00–22.00 Sat, 08.00–20.00 Sun ⓝ Bus: 2, 14, 15, 17, 19

⬥ *Kringlan Mall will keep you and your credit card entertained for hours*

Smáralind Mall Reykjavik's second mall opened to great fanfare despite its slightly out of the way location. More airy feeling inside than the older Kringlan Mall, Smáralind has a few international chains like Topshop that you won't find anywhere else in the city. ⓐ Hagasmári 1, 201 Kópavogur ⓣ 528 8000 ⓦ www.smaralind.is ⓛ 11.00–19.00 Mon– Fri, 11.00–18.00 Sat, 13.00–18.00 Sun ⓝ Bus: 2

TAKING A DIP

Árbæjarlaug Not far from Árbæjarsafn (see page 95), and with both indoor and outdoor pools, this spa also has a waterslide, sauna, solarium and steam bath. ⓐ Fylkisvegur, 110 ⓣ 510 7600 ⓛ 06.30–22.30 Mon–Fri, 08.00–20.30 Sat & Sun (until 22.00 Sat & Sun, Apr–Sept) ⓝ Bus: 19

Laugardalslaug Within the Laugardalur Valley sports area, these outdoor and indoor pools are the city's largest. Practise laps with professionals, or chat with locals. ⓐ Sundlaugavegur, 105 ⓣ 553 4039 ⓛ 06.30–22.00 Mon–Fri, 08.00–20.00 Sat & Sun (until 22.00 Sat & Sun, Apr–Sept) ⓝ Bus: 2, 14, 15, 17, 19

TAKING A BREAK

The cafés and restaurants listed below are shown on the main Reykjavik map on pages 58–9.

Árbæjarsafn £ ⓬ The outdoor museum has a delightful snack bar that serves waffles along with the usual range of coffees and ice creams. ⓐ Kistuhylur, 110 ⓣ 411 6300 ⓦ www.arbaejarsafn.is ⓛ 10.00–17.00 June–Aug ⓝ Bus: 19

Café Konditori Copenhagen £ ⑬ Close to Laugardalur Park is this Danish bakery chain that serves up gorgeous cakes, buttery croissants, and does a light breakfast and lunch buffet. ⓐ Suðurlandsbraut 4A, 108 ⓣ 588 1550 ⓦ www.konditori.is ⓒ 08.00–18.00 Mon–Fri, 09.00–17.00 Sat & Sun ⓝ Bus: 2, 14, 15, 17, 19

Kringlan Mall £ ⑭ The food court inside this giant shopping mall is perfect for keeping children happy, with all the fast-food chains and cafés you'd expect – plus a couple of Icelandic ones, such as Kaffitár coffee shop and the Boozt bar. ⓐ Kringlan 4–12, 103 ⓣ 517 9000 ⓦ www.kringlan.is ⓒ 10.00–18.30 Mon–Wed, 10.00–19.00 Thur & Fri, 10.00–18.00 Sat, 13.00–17.00 Sun ⓝ Bus: 1, 2, 3, 4, 6, 13, 14

Café Flora £–££ ⑮ The café inside Reykjavik Botanical Gardens (see page 90) is a fine spot in which to take a break after strolling through the flowers and shrubs. ⓐ Laugardalur Valley, 104 ⓣ 553 8872 ⓦ www.cafeflora.is ⓒ 10.00–22.00 May–Sept; 10.00–17.00 Oct–Apr ⓝ Bus: 2, 15, 17, 19

AFTER DARK

Virtually all of Reykjavik's after-dark action happens in the centre of town; the suburbs are very quiet. But if you do find yourself outside of the centre in the evening, then there are a couple of options:

RESTAURANTS

Lauga Ás £–££ ⑯ An old-fashioned family-run restaurant which has served up simple yet tasty fish and lobsters dishes for over three decades. ⓐ Laugarásvegur 1, 104 ⓣ 553 1620 ⓦ www.laugaas.is ⓒ 11.00–21.00 Mon–Fri, 15.00–21.00 Sat & Sun ⓝ Bus: 14

Vox ££–£££ ⑰ Inside the Hilton's Nordica Hotel you'll discover the Vox Bistro and Vox Restaurant – both a pleasure to visit, either for a decadent brunch at weekends or a smart dinner. Only Nordic ingredients are used. ⓐ Suðurlandsbraut 2, 108 ⓣ 444 5050 ⓦ www.vox.is ⓛ Restaurant: 18.30–22.30 Wed–Sat; bistro: 11.30–22.30 ⓝ Bus: 2, 14, 15, 17, 19

Grillið £££ ⑱ The granddaddy of Reykjavik fine dining is perched at the top of Hotel Saga with spectacular views of the city and sea, and is still decorated in the same stately style as it was 40 years ago when it first opened. The four-course 'Discovery Menu' is highly recommended. ⓐ Við Hagatorg, 107 ⓣ 525 9960 ⓦ www.grillid.is ⓛ 18.00–22.00 Tues–Sat ⓝ Bus: 11, 12 ❶ Closed for a month in summer; call to check exact dates

CINEMAS & THEATRES

The City Theatre Just next door to Kringlan Mall, this repertory theatre has four stages on which there are at least seven major projects annually, as well as several other smaller productions. The venue's programme includes everything from rock concerts to philosophical debates. ⓐ Listabraut 3, 103 ⓣ 568 8000 ⓦ www.borgarleikhus.is ⓛ Box office: 14.00–18.00 Tues & Wed, 14.00–20.00 Thur–Sat ⓝ Bus: 1, 2, 3, 4, 6, 13, 14

Sambíó Kringlan's cinema shows all the latest Hollywood films, some even before they've arrived in the UK. ⓐ Kringlan ⓦ www.kvikmyndir.is ⓛ Box office open 1 hr before performance ⓝ Bus: 1, 2, 3, 4, 6, 13, 14

❷ *If you are travelling away from the city, a visit to Geysir is a must*

OUT OF TOWN
trips

The Blue Lagoon & the Reykjanes Peninsula

Only about 50 km (31 miles) away from Reykjavik, and one of Iceland's biggest tourist attractions, is the Blue Lagoon. A huge pool brimming with the heated overspill from the nearby power plant, this enormous outdoor spa is supposed to be excellent for healing skin complaints and other ailments. Although a lazy day's activity in its own right, there are also many other things to see in the area.

Keflavík, nearby and better known for being the site of the international airport, offers whale-watching in the season. Grindavík is a small fishing village with a museum that pays tribute to what was once the country's biggest money earner, Icelandic salt cod. Further away, on some roads that might qualify as a driving adventure, are the dramatic cliffs of Krýsuvíkurberg. Not far from here is Seltún, site of a once energetic geyser, now a weird area of thermal pools and bubbling mud. Just before heading back to Reykjavik is Hafnarfjörður with its 'hidden' residents.

SIGHTS & ATTRACTIONS

The Blue Lagoon

On the way into Reykjavik from Keflavík International Airport, what looks like billowing white smoke rises above the fields of black lava. This plume is actually steam, and it comes from the nearby power station. Just next to it is the Blue Lagoon, the pool that gets its water from the plant. Many visitors stop en route to or from the airport to take a dip, and some tour operators' pick-up services schedule time here.

The Blue Lagoon is an artificial pool created when hot seawater was pumped out from the geothermally fuelled Svartsengi power plant, creating a lagoon. Running over the lava fields, the minerals within some of the water crystallised. Icelanders, being the thermal spa lovers that they are, started bathing in the pond. Psoriasis sufferers began to notice improvements in their skin when they rubbed some of the grainy white sludge onto the affected areas. In 1987 this therapy was acknowledged, and the first public pool opened. Gradually more facilities, such as medical staff and massage rooms, were incorporated into the spa. Now what once seemed to be mud is packaged as a skin product, sold at fine shops and sent all over the world. The spa has never been more popular.

The milky-turquoise blue water spreads over a huge area, surrounded by dark lava hills. Steam pumped from the centre of the pool rises up and, in the distance, a matching column rises from the source, the out-of-view power station. Within the lagoon are roped-off areas creating separate pools, as well as an energetic waterfall under which visitors can stand. Just next to them is a steam bath in what looks like a cave in the lava. Just beyond is a shallower pool where people can smear the white, healing mud all over their faces.

◗ *The milky water at the Blue Lagoon is reputed to have healing properties*

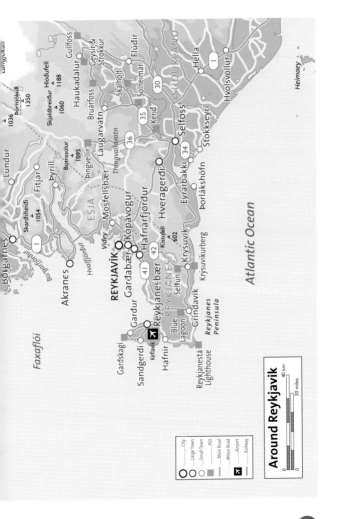

The Blue Lagoon is 16 km (10 miles) away from Keflavík and 48 km (30 miles) from Reykjavik. It takes approximately 20 minutes to drive from the airport. Airport taxis offer special rates for stopping at the lagoon on the way to or from Reykjavik, and most major tour operators offer Blue Lagoon tours. **Netbus** (Ⓦ www.bustravel.is) has several departures daily and offers a package that includes the Blue Lagoon's entry fee. Tours leave regularly from most hotels and guesthouses. ⓐ Grindavík ❶ 420 8800 Ⓦ www.bluelagoon.com ⓛ 08.00–21.00 June–Aug; 10.00–20.00 Sept–May

Garðskagi

At the northern tip of the Reykjanes Peninsula is the lighthouse at Garðskagi. Close to the town of Garður, there has been a beacon here since 1847, when a lamp was put on the top of a sign. A subsequent tower was built in 1897, but the one that's there now dates from 1944. During the migration periods of April–May and September–October, twitchers have a literal field day. To drive there, take route 41 west from Reykjavik. Just beyond Keflavík, turn north on route 45.

Grindavík

This seaside village is the Blue Lagoon's closest urban access. Though one of Iceland's most important fishing ports, tourism is beginning to play an important role and the town does have a few attractions in its own right. There are coastal walks as well as opportunities to path-find through the lava fields. For more organised sport, there's a nine-hole golf course. The Icelandic Saltfish Museum (see page 114) is Grindavík's tribute to the industry that put so many krónur into its pockets. To get there by car, take route 41 west till route 43, then go south. Ⓦ www.grindavik.is

ELVES

With a rich folklore that goes all the way back to the settlement of the country in the ninth century, elves, trolls and ghosts pervaded the Icelandic psyche. Now, with the interest in trolls receding, and electric light causing the demise of ghosts, elves remain a part of many Icelanders' lives. When questioned, locals may not vocalise their belief, but will admit that they wouldn't do anything to upset an elf. Documented cases exist of road builders who claim that when they moved a rock that was alleged to be an elf's home, all sorts of things went wrong. When they replaced it, suddenly everything was fine again.

Also known as the 'Hidden Folk', not many people are able to see the creatures. There are, however, acknowledged locations of their whereabouts, and Reykjavik's next-door neighbour, Hafnarfjörður, is supposed to be the home to the Royal Family of Elves. Apparently, the creatures show themselves only to those with second sight. 'Hidden Folk' do not live solely in the suburbs, however. Whenever anything disappears, or reappears in a strange place, especially after a long time, the Icelanders credit this as being of an elf's making.

Hafnarfjörður

Just 10 km (6 miles) from Reykjavik – a short ride on bus no. 1 – lies the so-called 'town in the lava'. Although most of the activity is on the flat area around the bay, the hills are constructed of the outflow from once-active volcanoes.

One of the highlights of the town is to see the charming, brightly coloured corrugated houses that have been built within the black

lava field. The harbour is lively and active, both small fishing craft and larger vessels moor here, and whale-watching trips leave from this area. Also nearby is the Ástjörn Nature Reserve, a haven for both walkers and birdwatchers (at the right time of year).

The quirkiest aspect of Hafnarfjörður is its reputation for having more 'hidden folk' or mythical creatures than any other area in the country. This arguable title is due mostly to the city's best known resident, the clairvoyant Erla Stefánsdóttir. Gifted with second sight, she offers tours to where the elves live. Alternatively, a map to these stars' homes is available at the tourist office.

Hafnarfjörður Tourist Office ⓐ Strandgata 6, Hafnarfjörður
ⓣ 585 5500 ⓦ www.hafnarfjordur.is ⓛ 08.00–17.00 Mon–Thur, 09.00–17.00 Fri, June–Aug ⓘ Tourist info point 11.00–17.00 Sat & Sun in Hafnarfjörður Museum (see page 113)

Krýsuvík

It's worth the trip to the thermal area of Krýsuvík-Seltún to see its strange hissing waters and bubbling mud pools. Although not far in terms of kilometres, it will take you longer than you think to get there: roads in this area are generally paved, but occasionally, and without warning, they turn into graded tracks. While rough, it is possible for an ordinary car with a careful driver to do the trip in fine weather. By car, head for Grindavík, then travel east on route 427. When it intersects with route 42, head north. For an easier journey back to Reykjavik, continue north on this road until it gets to route 41 at Hafnarfjörður.

Krýsuvíkurberg

This dramatic headland over the sea might require a bit of effort to reach, but it's definitely worth it. The cliff rises steeply over the sea, with a sweep straight down to the blue water below. The contrast

🔺 *Tread carefully near the boiling water and mud of Krýsuvík-Seltún*

against the dark sand is dramatic. In the summer, nesting birds crowd the place. From Grindavík, continue east on 427.

CULTURE

Garður Folk Museum
Within the lighthouse at the end of the peninsula, this little museum explains a bit about the folklore of the area. ⓐ Garðskagi Lighthouse, Garður ⓣ 422 7220 ⓛ 13.00–17.00 Apr–Oct

Hafnarfjörður Museum
Six historic houses make up this museum. Pakkhúsið contains exhibits which trace the history of the town since Viking days, plus a toy collection. Sívertsenshúsið depicts the life of an upper-class 19th-century family, while Siggubær is an example of a working-class home from the early 20th century. Bungalowið ('Bungalow') is the former home of Scottish fishing magnates the Bookless brothers and features an exhibition on fishing in the early 20th century. Beggubúð contains a Museum of Trade and Góðtemplarahúsið has an exhibition on the town's sporting history. ⓐ Vesturgata 8, Hafnarfjörður

❶ 585 5780 ❻ www.hafnarfjordur.is/byggdasafn ❸ Pakkhúsið: 11.00–
17.00 Fri–Wed, 11.00–21.00 Thur, June–Sept; 11.00–21.00 Thur, 11.00–
17.00 Sat & Sun, Oct–May. Sívertsenshúsið & Beggubúð: 11.00–17.00
June–Sept. Siggubær & Góðtemplarahúsið: 11.00–17.00 Sat & Sun,
June–Sept. Bungalowið: 10.00–17.00 June–Sept; 11.00–17.00 Sat & Sun,
Oct–Mar ❶ Visits possible during other times by appointment

Hidden Worlds Tour

Not your usual cultural attraction but interesting nevertheless:
guide Sigurbjörg Karlsdóttir takes visitors on a tour of where
the resident elves allegedly live, based on advice by clairvoyant
Erla Stefánsdóttir. ❸ Hafnarfjördur tourist office ❶ 694 2785
❻ www.alfar.is ❸ 14.30 Tues & Fri, other times by appointment

Icelandic Saltfish Museum

For a long time, producing salt fish (salted cod) was the biggest
business in Iceland. This museum depicts the history and importance
of the industry and shows how the export of this product proved to
be the financial foundation of modern Iceland. ❸ Hafnargata 12A,
Grindavík ❶ 420 1190 ❻ www.saltfisksetur.is ❸ 11.00–18.00

RETAIL THERAPY

Blue Lagoon shop Buy the same products that you wallow in, just
inside the main building. See page 106.

Fjörður Shopping Centre Comprises just about everything, including
fashion, toy, camera and jewellery stores, a bank, optician and
supermarket. ❸ Fjarðargata 13–15, Hafnarfjördur ❶ 565 5666
❸ 10.00–18.00 Mon–Thur, 10.00–19.00 Fri, 10.00–16.00 Sat

TAKING A DIP

Blue Lagoon For the biggest thermal pool of them all, see page 106.

Garður Swimming Centre A good place to soak away the exhaustion of a long day's touring. ❸ Garðbraut, Garður ❶ 422 7300 ❶ 07.00–21.00 Mon–Fri, 10.00–16.00 Sat & Sun, May–Aug

Keflavík Swimming Centre Close to the airport, with both a 25 m and a 50 m pool as well as the usual hot pots and steam bath. ❸ By Sunnubraut, Reykjanesbær ❶ 421 1500 ❶ 06.45–21.00 Mon–Fri, 08.00–18.00 Sat & Sun, May–Aug; 08.00–18.00 Sat & Sun, Sept–Apr

Suðurbæjarlaug The outside pool is only part of the complex, with Nautilus gym, solarium and massages, as well as the ubiquitous hot pots and steam bath. ❸ Hringbraut 77, Hafnarfjörður ❶ 565 3080 ❶ 06.30–21.30 Mon–Fri, 08.00–18.30 Sat, 08.00–17.30 Sun

Sundhöll Hafnarfjörður The pool is indoors, but the hot pots are outdoors. Linger in the sauna, too. ❸ Herjólfsgata 10, Hafnarfjörður ❶ 555 0088 ❶ 06.30–21.00 Mon–Fri, 08.00–12.00 Sat & Sun. Women's night: Tues, Thur 20.00–21.00

TAKING A BREAK & AFTER DARK

Café Aroma £ Here is a place to drop your shopping bags, rest a bit and grab some caffeine. ❸ Fjörður Shopping Centre, Hafnarfjörður ❶ 555 6996 ❶ 10.00–00.00 Mon–Wed, 10.00–01.00 Thur, 10.00–03.00 Fri & Sat, 13.00–00.00 Sun

Fjörukráin £ A Viking-themed restaurant, in which waiters dressed in Viking costume serve up platters of fish or lamb and jugs of ale. Kitsch but fun. ⓐ Strandgata 55, Hafnarfjörður ⓣ 565 1213 ⓦ www.fjorukrain.is ⓛ 18.00–01.00

Mamma Mía Pizzahús £ A quick stop if you're passing through Grindavík and you need a bite. ⓐ Hafnargata 7A, Grindavík ⓣ 426 9966 ⓛ 17.00–22.00 Mon–Fri, 12.00–22.00 Sat & Sun

Fjöruborðið ££ Serving South Iceland's best lobster soup, this is a great place to stop after a long day sightseeing in the countryside. ⓐ Eyrarbraut 3A, Stokkseyri ⓣ 483 1550 ⓦ www.fjorubordid.is ⓛ 12.00–21.00 Sun–Thur, 12.00–22.00 Fri–Sat

Lava ££ The Blue Lagoon spa (see page 106) has an excellent restaurant with an international menu, where you can eat while watching the bathers. ⓐ Grindavík ⓣ 420 8806 ⓦ www.bluelagoon.com ⓛ 11.30–21.00 June–Aug; 11.30–20.30 Sept–May

The Red House ££ In the little village of Eyrarbakki on the coast near Grindavík, this bright and airy restaurant housed in a historic building serves Icelandic lobster and a simple menu of fresh, nicely presented dishes. ⓐ Búðarstígur 4, Eyrarbakki ⓣ 483 3330 ⓦ www.raudahusid.is ⓛ 11.30–21.00 Sun–Thur, 11.30–22.00 Fri & Sat

Salthúsið ££ Specialising in salt fish, 'The Salt House' serves up hearty Icelandic fare in atmospheric surroundings. Kids love the play area, complete with toys and colouring books. ⓐ Stamphólsvegur 2, Grindavík ⓣ 426 9700 ⓦ www.salthusid.is ⓛ 17.00–22.00 Mon–Fri, 12.30–00.00 Sat, 12.30–22.00 Sun (kitchen closes 21.00)

ACCOMMODATION

Fit Hostel £ Near the international airport, this youth hostel has sleeping, cooking and bathing facilities, including a hot tub in summer. ⓐ Fitjabraut 6A/6B, Njarðvík ❶ 421 8889

Northern Light Inn ££ The closest place to stay to the Blue Lagoon, the hotel offers comfortable accommodation with all facilities. ⓐ Grindavíkurbraut 1, Grindavík ❶ 426 8650 ⓦ www.northernlightinn.is

Blue Lagoon Clinic ££–£££ A little-known fact is that rooms can be rented in the beautifully designed Blue Lagoon skin clinic near the famous blue waters open to the public. The separate facility is only a five-minute walk from the main spa, and features clean, graceful rooms with a view of the volcanic lava fields. An isolated, peaceful place to stay. ⓐ Grindavík ❶ 420 8806 ⓦ www.bluelagoon.com

Hótel Keflavík £££ This 4-star hotel is a good place to stay if you're looking for luxurious accommodation. ⓐ Vatnsnesvegur 12–14, Reykjanesbær ❶ 420 7000 ⓦ www.kef.is

CAMPSITES
Garður Camping ⓐ Garður ❶ 422 7220 ⓦ www.sv-gardur.is

Grindavík Camping ⓐ Grindavík ❶ 420 1190 ⓦ www.grindavik.is

Keflavík Airport Motel rooms and sleeping-bag accommodation are also available. ❶ 421 2800 ⓦ www.alex.is

The Golden Circle

Probably the most popular and certainly the most attended day excursion out of Reykjavik is the Golden Circle. This tour is a sort of taster of Iceland, offering a view of many of the country's varied landscapes within a relatively short period of time. It is also possible to do the trip independently, as all the roads are on paved or well-graded roads. The return trip is around 250 km (155 miles).

The first stop is Þingvellir, the site of the world's first Parliament in AD 930 as well as the Great Atlantic Rift. From there the standard tour continues to Geysir, the original shooting hot spring that gave its name to similar phenomena around the world. The scenery changes suddenly as volcanic lava takes over. Visible by its rising mist long before it comes into view, the magnificent waterfall Gullfoss plunges down a deep chasm, one of Iceland's most memorable sites. On extended tours, there's a chance to pass the falls on a four-wheel-drive track to get to the glacier Langjökull and do some skidooing on the snow.

SIGHTS & ATTRACTIONS

Geysir

In a delightful region of farmland and summer green fields, the land suddenly turns red and the whiff of rotten eggs is noticeable. Also apparent are the tour buses and advertisements for the café and hotel. Out of nowhere, steam seems to rise out of the earth and, if the timing is right, a huge column of water spurts up into the sky.

Geysir is the name of one of the geysers in this small but impressive hot spring area. Erupting only after an earthquake (the last one in 2000), the plumes are supposed to reach up to 80 m (262 ft). Still, its next-door neighbour, the little but more reliable

◆ *The geyser at Strokkur puts on a show every five minutes or so*

Strokkur, is pretty much why people continue to flock to this tourist attraction and natural wonder. At intervals of about five minutes, the geyser regularly shoots up 25–30 m (70–100 ft) into the air. The process, and anticipation, are fascinating. After an eruption, the water starts draining slowly back into the geyser's basin, rising and falling like breathing. It threatens to blow, then pulls the water back several times, the number depending on how high the last eruption was. Finally, a turquoise-blue bubble forms on the surface and suddenly hot water shoots high into the air. Sometimes there are a few little explosions surrounding the big one, although each expulsion is different. The perimeter of Strokkur is marked off, and puddles indicate which way the wind is blowing. Stay out of this area to avoid getting soaked, even though the warm water is pleasant (until it grows cold!).

Other smaller springs bubble away, and it's possible to walk around or up the hill to get a good view. Despite the ease of access and the general friendly tone, extreme caution must be exercised here. The water is hot and the earth thin, and it's possible to break through it into boiling water. Stick to the designated paths, even if it's tempting to wander outside of these borders. There is no admission charge to the thermal area. Across the street is a tourist complex, with a café, hotel and other facilities. There is also a folk museum and a multimedia show on the geology of the region.

Gullfoss

The land becomes barren and volcanic, and just about 10 km (6 miles) further northeast of Geysir, what seems to be fog rises out of the black land. In contrast to Geysir, almost nothing is visible and a

● *The views over the falls at Gullfoss are breathtaking*

small sign points to a parking area for Gullfoss. Arguably Iceland's prettiest waterfall, these incredible chutes have several viewpoints, all dramatic in their own right. Past the low-key café and shop, a path leads to an overview. In sunshine, a huge rainbow hangs over the water, a product of wind blowing the spray. The arc moves as the angle of the sun shifts.

On overcast days, the falls are still extraordinary, and the raw sense of power seems to come through more clearly. Walking down the steps, it's possible to stroll along the west bank of the Hvítá River and its 2.5 km (1.5 miles) canyon towards the main falls. The lower cascade drops about 22 m (72 ft) and the upper 11 m (35 ft), but it's not the height that's impressive – rather the shape of the canyon and the amount of water pushing through. The trail leads to rocks that jut out between the two sections, and it's worth looking back along the main drop to get an impression of the sheer volume of water. A further path goes up the hill away from the falls, but grants a good overview of the area.

Langjökull Glacier

Langjökull is the country's second-largest ice field (after Vatnajökull in the east). With an area of around 950 sq km (590 miles), its elevation varies between 1,200 and 1,500 m (4,000 and 5,500 ft). The glacier is four-wheel-drive accessible from mountain (F) tracks. The road that continues from Gullfoss is probably the easiest way to get there, although extreme caution is advised. It's strongly advised that you visit the glacier only with an organised tour as the locals know the best access points and are aware of the latest weather conditions. Glaciers are extremely dangerous, especially in falling snow, which happens at any time of the year. Light drifts cover up fragile crevasses and deep water holes, and even the most powerful vehicles can get stuck.

Nonetheless, a visit to Langjökull on a tour, often en route from the Golden Circle, is a lot of fun. Many companies, including **Activity Group** (Ⓦ www.activity.is), **Reykjavik Excursions** (Ⓦ www.re.is), **Iceland Excursions** (Ⓦ www.icelandexcursions.is) and **Mountain Taxi** (Ⓦ www.mountaintaxi.is), offer SuperJeep expeditions on the glacier. Some include snowmobiles or skidoos as part of the tour. Not quite as easy as they look but still fine for first-timers, gliding along on the glaciers via one of these modified motorbikes is great to try. It's certainly the best way to see as much as possible in the time allotted. The tours are carefully escorted and, within the framework of adventure tourism, relatively safe.

Þingvellir

A designated national park and point of national reverence as well as a UNESCO Heritage Site, Þingvellir is an eerie and extraordinary place. The first view coming from the west and south is from the visitor centre perched on a hill over the site. Looking down into a large depression, a lake is visible to the south (Þingvallavatn). In the far distance is a large wall rising up, matched by the one on which the visitor centre stands. In the middle is a meadow area with rivers running through and a few interesting-looking buildings with pointed roofs. Jagged lines of rock zigzag through the area.

This area is the location of the Great Atlantic Rift, the point on the planet where the North American and Eurasian tectonic plates are separating. Essentially, this is where Europe and America come together, although their meeting point is dividing at a rate of 2 cm a year. The large valley below, between the walls, is new earth, growing larger every day and is considered by some to be 'no man's land', an area of neither one continent nor the other. Some locals feel that this new

◆ Þingvellir is the scenic home of the first Parliament

land should be an area of independent government, but Icelandic officials have incorporated this spot as one of national importance.

Þingvellir is also the site that the Vikings selected for their Alþingi in AD 930, the general assembly and the first Parliament in recorded history. Equally accessible from most of the settlements of the period, the local chiefs came here to resolve their arguments. Stories fly about the behaviour of these Nordic lords, ranging from how they resolved their disputes by duels to how they settled their differences by bribery. Apparently, bad behaviour by women was not tolerated; there is a legendary spot in the extremely cold glacial run-off river where wayward females were quickly dealt with, whether by drowning or freezing, as punishment. More documented is the location of the actual assembly, the Law Rock (Lögberg), where natural acoustics allowed whoever was speaking to be heard. Nothing remains of the original assembly, but the spot is commemorated by a flag, flying next to the church (a 1907 reconstruction of the original built in AD 1000).

Also on the site is Þingvallabær, the summer residence of the country's Prime Minister in the form of a traditional farmhouse, built for the 1,000-year anniversary of the foundation of the Alþingi.

CULTURE

Geysir Centre at Geysir

Across the street from the thermal area is the complex that includes the Geysirstofa, a multimedia show that has a changing programme of Iceland's natural phenomena. Also here is an earthquake simulator, and a folk museum on the upper floors. ⓐ Geysir ☏ 480 6800 ⓦ www.geysircenter.com ⏰ 10.00–19.00 May–Sept; 11.00–17.00 Oct; 12.00–17.00 Nov & Dec; 12.00–16.00 Jan & Feb; 12.00–17.00 Mar; 11.00–17.00 Apr

Sólheimar

Sólheimar A slight detour off the road to Geysir is a very special eco-community where Icelanders with special needs live with Icelanders who chose to reside in this unique, diverse eco-topia. Stop by for some of the cafe's organic cooking, and buy some vegetables grown in the garden or one of the beautiful crafts made by residents in their workshops. ⓐ Sólheimar Eco Village, Selfoss ☏ 480 4400 ⓦ www.solheimar.is

Þingvellir Visitor Centre

The first place to go when visiting the site, the visitor centre has

displays, a 3D relief map and probably the best overlook of the national park. ⓐ Þingvellir National Park, near campsite ❶ 482 2660 ⓦ www.thingvellir.is ❷ 09.00–17.00 Apr & May; 09.00–19.00 June–Aug; 09.00–17.00 Sept & Oct; 09.00–17.00 Sat & Sun, Nov–Mar

RETAIL THERAPY

Geysir Centre A surprisingly comprehensive souvenir store exists in this tourist facility, in case there's still something needed after shopping in Reykjavik. It's also possible to buy edibles for a picnic lunch in the snack shop. ⓐ Geysir ❶ 480 6800 ⓦ www.geysircenter.com ❷ 10.00–20.00 May–Sept; 10.00–17.00 Mar, Apr & Oct; 10.00–16.00 Nov–Feb

Gullfoss Overlooking the falls is a fairly well supplied shop that sells the usual tourist goods. ⓐ Gullfoss

Selfoss Just south of the Golden Circle and a handy stop-off on the way back to Reykjavik on route 1 is Selfoss. The largest town in the area, with a population of over 7,000, it has a large range of facilities, including a few good bakeries and two large supermarkets.

TAKING A DIP

Hótel Geysir The hotel across from the thermal area has a 17.5 m (60 ft) swimming pool open to the public in the summer. The adjoining hot tubs are open all year round. ⓐ Geysir ❶ 480 6800 ⓦ www.geysircenter.com ❷ 15 Apr–1 Sept; hot tubs all year

Hótel Gullfoss The hotel has a hot tub on the deck for its guests. ⓐ Brattholt, Bláskógabyggð, near Gullfoss ⓣ 486 8979 ⓦ www.hotelgullfoss.is

Laugarvatn Swimming Pool On the road between Þingvellir and Geysir is the thermal resort town of Laugarvatn. Steam seems to come from everywhere, and it's possible to indulge in it, via the 25 m (80 ft) swimming pool and its three hot pots. ⓐ Laugarvatn ⓣ 486 1251 ⓛ 10.00–22.00 Mon–Fri, 10.00–18.00 Sat & Sun, summer; 17.00–20.00 Mon–Fri, 13.00–17.00 Sat & Sun, winter

Selfoss The swimming pool is designed for the whole family. There's also a sauna. ⓐ Bankavegur, Selfoss ⓣ 480 1960 ⓦ www.arborg.is ⓛ 06.45–21.30 Mon–Fri, 09.00–20.00 Sat & Sun, summer; 08.00–20.00 Sat, winter

TAKING A BREAK

Geysir Centre £ The snack shop has standard fare, including hamburgers, chips, pizza and hotdogs and ordinary coffee. ⓐ Geysir ⓣ 480 6800 ⓦ www.geysircenter.com ⓛ 10.00–20.00 May–Sept; 10.00–17.00 Mar, Apr & Oct; 10.00–16.00 Nov–Feb

Gullfoss £ Getting out of the spray that pervades the area, the restaurant here is pretty decent. The Icelandic lamb stew is particularly satisfying on a cold wet day (with one free refill included). When the sky is clear, the outdoor deck is a great sun trap. ⓐ Gullfoss ⓣ 486 6500 ⓦ www.gullfoss.is ⓛ 09.00–17.00 or 18.00 winter; 09.00–21.30 summer

AFTER DARK

Not much goes on in the countryside outside of the hotels.

Hótel Geysir £ Right across from the geysers, this restaurant offers an international menu featuring Icelandic specialities sourced directly from farmers in the region. See below for contact details. 🕐 08.00–21.00

Hótel Gullfoss £ winter, **££** summer. Native cuisine is prepared country-style at the in-house restaurant but more than that, it's convenient for the nearby attractions. See below for contact details. 🕐 19.00–21.00

Riverside Restaurant ££ at Hótel Selfoss. One of the best venues in the area, the restaurant serves creative versions of some classic dishes. There is also a daily fixed-price menu. See page 129 for contact details. 🕐 12.00–22.00

ACCOMMODATION

HOTELS

Hótel Geysir £ without facilities, **££** en suite. The Geysir Centre has luxury cabins, cheaper ordinary rooms and a campsite, as well as a playground for kids. Get up early in the morning and watch Strokkur erupt without anyone else around. ⓐ Geysir ① 480 6800 ⓦ www.geysircenter.com

Hótel Gullfoss ££ summer, **£** winter. This friendly hotel in a very quiet rural location has 16 rooms with full facilities. ⓐ Brattholt, Bláskógabyggð, near Gullfoss ① 486 8979 ⓦ www.hotelgullfoss.is

Hótel Selfoss ££ A luxury hotel with everything a 4-star lodging should have, and it's picturesquely located right next to the same roaring river that falls through Gullfoss upstream. ⓐ Eyrarvegur 2, Selfoss ⓣ 480 2500 ⓦ www.hotelselfoss.is

HOSTELS

Arnes £ This youth hostel is about 42 km (26 miles) northeast of Selfoss, and well situated for what there is to see in the vicinity. A swimming pool and restaurant are nearby. In the summer there are regular bus connections to Reykjavik. From Selfoss, go east on route 30, then north on route 32 approximately 14 km. ⓐ Gnúpverjahreppur, Selfoss ⓣ 486 6048 ⓦ www.hihostels.com

Laugarvatn £ Located in the village, this youth hostel has rooms with shared facilities for up to six people, as well as new en suite rooms. There is a kitchen and hot tub, and staff can arrange boat rentals and mountain jeep tours. ⓐ Dalsel, Laugarvatn ⓣ 486 1215 ⓦ www.hihostels.com

CAMPSITES

There are lots of campsites in the area. The closest to Golden Circle attractions are Hótel Geysir's camping facilities and:

Þingvellir National Park Camping Ground Two areas in the park allow camping. At Leirar just a five-minute walk from the Information Centre, there are four different sites, Fagrabrekka, Syðri-Leirar, Hvannabrekka and Nyrðri-Leirar. Further away, at Lake Þingvallavatn, is Vatnskot. Ask at the Information Centre for details and permits. ⓐ Selfoss ⓣ 482 2660 ⓦ www.thingvellir.is

Snæfellsnes Peninsula

On a clear day, looking northwest across the bay from Reykjavik, it's possible to make out the far distant image of a picture-perfect volcano. Rising up in a classic shape, covered with a white crown all year round, this mountain is topped by its glacier. Jules Verne used this location as the entrance to his *Journey to the Centre of the Earth*, and New Agers believe it is one of the earth's most powerful energy points.

The peak is about 200 km (125 miles) away by car from the capital, and rests at the end of another of Iceland's beautiful and easily accessible peninsulas. Within the jurisdiction of a national park, the massif and its glacier are reached either via an organised tour (see Arnarstapi, page 132) or independently (see Snæfellsjökull, page 133). Nearby are lovely – and sometimes lava-blackened – sea-swept beaches. To the north is the charming fishing village of Stykkishólmur and, further west, the commercial port of Ólafsvík. The local waters here are yet another stomping ground for visiting sea mammals, including their largest representative, the blue whale. Scattered among the fields, sometimes for no apparent reason, are little churches, particularly prominent against the sweeping mountain backdrop. Most of these are open and can be entered, and if not, the local farm resident usually has the key.

Note that, in these remote parts, opening times of shops, restaurants, cafés and even swimming pools vary depending on the season, the weather, and the whims of the owner. If you are planning to make a special trip somewhere, it's advisable to call in advance to avoid disappointment.

◉ *Don't let the name 'Garbage Bay' stop you visiting Dritvik*

SIGHTS & ATTRACTIONS

Arnarstapi

This small fishing hamlet nestles comfortably under Snæfellsjökull mountain, from which it gains its most important source of income. Snowmobile and skidoo tours up to the glacier are offered from here, when there is enough snow on which to play (🔘 www.snjofell.is). When there isn't, a four-wheel-drive road through to Ólafsvík, on the north side of the peninsula, passes by its toe. Again, extreme caution is advised when venturing onto the ice. The 8 km (5 mile) walk to the next village of Hellnar, hiking through the lava fields along the rugged coast, is not as daunting as it sounds, and a pleasure on a long summer evening.

Several species of seabird overwhelm the area in the season, and a large Arctic tern colony is resident in the village. During nesting times the birds are everywhere, but pay due attention to their cautionary cries, as they can attack if they feel their chicks are threatened and will ruin a nice walk if they're out in full force.

Búðir

Just off the junction of roads 54 and 574, this beautiful tidal estuary, with its golden beach, rests at the end of an impressive lava field. Only a little church and a small luxury hotel are here. Nevertheless, the 19th-century church is charming, in a traditional wooden style, and the accommodation absolutely first class.

This is a delightful spot to get away from most of civilisation, enjoying the sea air and mountain views, while still wallowing in the luxury of an excellent resort.

Djúpalónssandur & Dritvík

Now part of Snæfellsjökull National Park, Djúpalónssandur was once a thriving fishing port. The only reminders that this place was ever anything other than an empty beach are a few pieces of rusty metal strewn among the black stones. These remnants are the nautical equivalent of dried bleached bones, from shipwrecks of the past. A bit further along, past four increasingly large stones, the lifting of which is said to measure strength, is Dritvík ('Garbage Bay') a lovely horseshoe bay with a dark beach. The pebbles here are shiny and have been rounded by the sea, and are known as black pearls by the locals.

Flatey Island

The 19th-century village on Flatey is a nice detour and only an 80-minute ferry ride out of the harbour at Stykkishólmur. (There are a few Flatey Islands off the coast of Iceland; this one is in Breiðafjörður Bay.) During summer, you can spend the night at the seasonal **Hótel Flatey** (Ⓦ www.hotelflatey.is), or just stop over for an afternoon stroll around town to see the local puffin hunters at work.

Grundarfjörður

A small fishing village on the north coast of Snafellsnes, Grundarfjörður sits right in the midst of some of the most odd and striking mountains in Iceland. The largest sticks out like a huge horn into the fjord, covered in green moss in the summer. This is a great place to stop for a night, have a quiet meal downtown, and get up early to commune with the sheep on the hiking trails.

Snæfellsjökull

On clear days, this magnificent mountain can be visible for hundreds of kilometres. With a height of only 1,446 m (4,744 ft), and a glacier only a fraction of the size of the country's larger ice fields, this mountain nevertheless has special significance to Icelanders.

Believed to be mystical by both locals and New Age travellers, the archetypal cone was briefly believed to be a landing site for extraterrestrials (who never appeared). Even Jules Verne imagined the indentation at the top to be the entrance to the planet's core, inspiring his 1864 novel, *Journey to the Centre of the Earth*. Whether more empowered than any other of Iceland's magical sites or not, the geography of the area is stunning. Rising from the sea and providing a striking backdrop to almost anywhere in Snæfellsnes, it's not surprising that magical powers have been attributed to this area.

The summit of the glacier can be reached on foot, via three routes. The first two options involve taking the F (mountain) 570 road, which runs from north to south from Olafsvik to Arnarstapi and passes close to the base of the ice. With a four-wheel-drive vehicle, the road can usually be reached from either town, although snow can block the pass. There are two tracks off this route that lead to the top.

The other way up leaves from the tiny fishing village of Hellisandur to the northwest of the peninsula following the 574 ring road. There is an unnamed four-wheel-drive track about 4 km (2½ miles) inland that heads east then south towards the mountain. At the end of the road, the path heads up, eventually reaching the ice, then the peak. Glacier hiking can be very dangerous, and unless hikers are extremely experienced and knowledgeable about crossing these surfaces, a better alternative might be to take a snowmobile tour from Arnarstapi (see page 132).

Stykkishólmur

Snæfellsnes' 'capital' is a delightful fishing town with a population of about 1,200. Corrugated iron buildings of various colours nestle against a lively harbour, which is backed up against a lighthouse-topped cliff. The view from the top of the crag to the south overlooks

◯ *Stykkishólmur is a small but charming town in a dramatic setting*

the harbour and the mountains, and, to the north, the Breiðafjörður Bay. A ferry runs from Stykkishólmur across the water past the historic island of Flatey to the North West Fjord region.

The town has quite a few facilities for tourists, including a craft shop, café and restaurant. The district museum is located in the Nordic House, while the space-age-looking church on the hill occasionally presents concerts open to the public. Nature-watching excursions, offered by **Seatours** (ⓦ www.seatours.is), take visitors out for trips in Breiðafjörður Bay. Nearby, horse riding is available, and there's even a nine-hole golf course close to the Hótel Stykkishólmur.

CULTURE

Búðir Church

Off a dirt road towards the sea, just past the Hótel Búðir, is the charming Búðir Church. Although some sort of religious edifice has been here since the early 18th century, this wooden building was built in 1847. Even though it's small, the church is still frequently used, often by couples wanting to get married in such a beautiful spot. ⓐ Heading west, turn south off route 574 on to an ungraded road (signposted Búðir), about 0.5 km (0.3 miles) after the junction with route 54

Gamla Pakkhúsið (The Old Warehouse)

Ólafsvík's past is portrayed in photographs and exhibits located in this 19th-century timber warehouse. Not surprisingly for such an important commercial port, the story of the area's fishing is featured. ⓐ Gamla Pakkhúsið, Ólafsvík ❶ 433 6930 🕐 11.00–17.00 end May–early Sept

Hellnar Church

Another of the small churches, this 1945 construction is notable for its incredible location, just beneath Snæfellsjökull. The building is a good point of reference on the Arnarstapi to Hellnar coastal walk.
🄰 Just north of the centre of the village

Norska Húsið (Nordic House)

Situated within a large Norwegian-style wooden building, the museum describes Stykkishólmur's local history. 🄰 Hafnargata 5, Stykkishólmur ❶ 438 1640 🄲 11.00–17.00 June–Aug; by arrangement Sept–May

Stykkishólmur Church

Prominently situated on a hill overlooking the sea, this modern-looking church is worth a visit both for the view and in order to see the gorgeous mural inside. 🄰 Stykkishólmur ❶ 438 1560

RETAIL THERAPY

Most shops are in the larger villages, although service stations usually include small eateries or shops selling the basics.

SERVICE STATIONS (BENSÍNSTÖÐ)

Arnarbær 🄰 Arnarstapi ❶ 435 6783 🄲 Restaurant: 08.00–23.00; petrol: 24 hrs
Ólís 🄰 Aðalgata 25, Stykkishólmur ❶ 438 1254 🄲 08.00–23.00
Söluskáli OK Fast food 🄰 Ólafsbraut 27, Ólafsvík ❶ 436 1012 🄲 09.00–23.00 Mon–Sat, 10.00–23.00 Sun

ÓLAFSVÍK

Apótek Ólafsvíkur Ólafsvík's pharmacy has most of the supplies

usually found at a chemist. ⓐ Ólafsbraut 24, Ólafsvík ⓣ 436 1261
ⓛ 10.00–12.30, 14.00–18.00

Blómaverk Even in Iceland, flowers are regular gifts. ⓐ Ólafsbraut 24,
Ólafsvík ⓣ 436 1688 ⓛ 13.00–16.00 Mon–Fri, 14.00–18.00 Sat

TAKING A DIP

Pool opening times vary depending on the weather and season.
It's advisable to call before visiting.

Grundarfjörður Swimming Pool ⓐ Borgarbraut, Grundarfjörður
ⓣ 438 8564
Lýsuhóll Swimming Pool A special pool with algae that locals swear
by for its restorative qualities. Not for the squeamish. ⓐ On the road
to Búðir ⓣ 435 6716
Ólafsvík Swimming Pool ⓐ Einnisbraut 11, Ólafsvík ⓣ 433 9910
Stykkishólmur Swimming Pool ⓐ Borgarbraut 4, Stykkishólmur
ⓣ 433 8150

TAKING A BREAK

Brauðgerðarhús Stykkishólms £ The town bakery provides snacks
and goodies. Look out for 'love balls' – an Icelandic donut generally
only found in bakeries outside the city. ⓐ Nesvegur 1, Stykkishólmur
ⓣ 438 1830 ⓛ Times vary, summer only

Fjöruhúsið Hellnar £ One of the best little cafés you'll ever find, serving
delicious seafood soup in a tiny, old Icelandic house tucked into the
cliffs at the edge of town. ⓐ Hellnar ⓣ 435 6844 ⓛ Times vary

● *Some of the rooms in Hótel Búðir offer great views of Snæfellsjökull*

Narfeyrarstofa £ An elegant, atmospheric small café near the harbour, serving fish soup with fresh seafood from Breiðafjörður, just a stone's throw away. ❸ Aðalgata 3, Stykkishólmur ❶ 438 1119

AFTER DARK

Fimm fiskar £ Fish and pizza in a corrugated iron building in town. ❷ Frúarstígur 4, Stykkishólmur ❶ 436 1600

Krákan £–££ This friendly, family-run restaurant serves delicious fresh fish and a mean plate of Icelandic lamb, complete with the traditional accompanying sauces that you won't find in the big city. It gets lively on weekend nights when locals stop in to have a drink or three. ❸ Sæból 13, Grundarfjörður ❶ 438 6499

ACCOMMODATION

Snjófell £ The little village has a large campsite equipped with toilet and shower blocks. ⓐ Arnarstapi ❶ 435 6783 ⓦ www.snjofell.is

Youth Hostel Grundarfjörður £ An inexpensive, friendly option for bunk or sleeping-bag accommodation along the peninsula's northern coast. Private and multiple bunk rooms available; book a cheaper bed off-season and you may have a whole room of bunks to yourself. ⓐ Hliðarvegur 15, Grundarfjörður ❶ 562 6533 ⓦ www.hihostels.com

Hótel Breiðarfjörður ££ Family-run hotel with 12 rooms. ⓐ Aðalgata 8, Stykkishólmur ❶ 433 2200 ⓦ http://hotelbreidafjordur.is

Hótel Hellnar ££ An eco hotel that's cheaper and mellower than upmarket Búðir, but missing none of the fabulous location overlooking the sea under the gaze of the glacier. ⓐ Brekkubær Hellnar, Snæfellsbær ❶ 435 6820 ⓦ www.hellnar.is

Hótel Búðir £££ In a wonderful location by a lava field next to the sea, Snæfellsjökull is visible from most of the deluxe rooms, though no. 11, the master suite, has the best view. ⓐ Búðir ❶ 435 6700 ⓦ www.budir.is

Hótel Glymur £££ Ideally located by the Hvalfjörður fjord and the beautiful Glymur waterfall, Hótel Glymur is a friendly, family-run hotel with a decent restaurant. ⓐ Hvalförður ❶ 430 3100 ⓦ www.hotelglymur.is

● *All roads lead to Reykjavik*

PRACTICAL
information

Directory

GETTING THERE

As Iceland is an island in the North Atlantic, the only ways of getting there are by air and sea.

By air

From the UK, two scheduled airlines fly to Reykjavik all year round: **Icelandair** (ⓦ www.icelandair.co.uk) and the low-cost **Iceland Express** (ⓦ www.icelandexpress.com). Icelandair has regular flights from various airports on the east coast of the United States and Canada as well as several cities in Europe. The airline also offers stopover packages in Reykjavik on transatlantic routes. Iceland Express flies to 17 European destinations in summer, but only six in winter.

During the summer, other airlines and charter operators ply the route, often in conjunction with package tours.

Many people are aware that air travel emits CO_2, which contributes to climate change. You may be interested in the possibility of lessening the environmental impact of your flight through the charity **Climate Care** (ⓦ www.climatecare.org), which offsets your CO_2 by funding environmental projects around the world.

By water

Smyril Line (ⓦ www.smyril-line.com) is the only regularly scheduled ferry that operates all year. It runs from Denmark to the Faeroe Islands, before arriving at the eastern Iceland port of Seyðisfjörður. During the summer, various cruise lines include a stopover in Reykjavik as part of their Arctic routes.

🔻 *Your last glimpse of Reykjavik will probably be something like this*

Package deals

You can often get good value deals by booking a package tour which includes flights, accommodation and transfers. **Discover the World** (☎ +44 1737 218 810 🌐 www.discover-the-world.co.uk) is one of the most experienced operators in this region and can offer a range of options. Both Icelandair and Iceland Express (see opposite) also offer package deals.

ENTRY FORMALITIES

Visas are not required for passport holders from Australia, Canada, New Zealand, Republic of Ireland, United Kingdom and United States. South African citizens must obtain visas before arrival.

As a participant in the Schengen agreement, travellers from other countries within the group do not, in principle, need to show documents. However, it is always advisable to travel with a passport or identity card.

The following customs limits are in place at the time of writing:

Food The import of up to 3 kg of food is allowed, as long as the value is not more than 18,500Kr.

Alcoholic beverages If you plan to import alcohol into Iceland duty-free, pick one of the following options: 1 litre of spirits and 1 litre of wine; 1 litre of spirits and 6 litres of beer; 1.5 litres of wine and 6 litres of beer; 3 litres of wine. The minimum age for bringing alcoholic beverages into Iceland is 20 years.

Tobacco 200 cigarettes or 250 g of other tobacco products. The minimum age for bringing tobacco into Iceland is 18 years.

Angling gear, riding gear and clothing which has been used outside Iceland, including gloves, boots and waders, may be brought into the country if it has been disinfected according to valid regulations. A certificate of disinfection, issued by an authorised veterinary officer, will be acceptable if presented to customs. If such a certificate is not presented, the gear has to be disinfected at the possessor's own cost on arrival.

For more information, check ⓦ www.tollur.is

MONEY

The Icelandic currency is the króna (plural krónur). The usual notation for Icelandic currency is ISK or Kr. Notes are in the following denominations: 500, 1,000, 2,000 and 5,000; while coins are in values of 1, 10, 50 and 100. It is advisable to change currency within the country, and change back before leaving, as foreign banks do not often deal with krónur.

Generally, though, large amounts of cash are unnecessary, as credit cards can be used for almost any amount, even relatively small

TAX-FREE SHOPPING

Iceland participates in a tax-free scheme and offers a refund of up to 15 per cent for tourists off a minimum purchase of 4,000Kr. After the completion of all purchases, go to the tourist office and claim the refund. The tax will be refunded in cash, but a credit card will be requested for security. You can also go to the desk in the departures lounge of Keflavík Airport.

ones. Icelanders accept most cards, although the most commonly used are MasterCard and Visa.

There are ATM machines in every town, and they accept Visa and MasterCard, as well as Cirrus and Maestro. Traveller's cheques are becoming less common, but can be changed at any bank.

HEALTH, SAFETY & CRIME

Iceland is one of the cleanest and safest countries in Europe, if not, indeed, the world. Fresh, running water is one of the nation's most important assets, and it's fine to drink it from almost any source, including taps. Bottled water is available, but it usually comes from the same place as the domestic supply.

In summer, insects can be a problem – Lake Mývatn means 'midge lake' for a reason. Although the bugs carry no diseases and are not dangerous, they can be very annoying. Taking along a decent insect repellent is recommended.

Temperatures can drop dramatically throughout the year, and it's a good idea to carry enough clothing to keep warm and waterproof, even during the summer. For weather information, see ⓦ http://en.vedur.is. Decent hiking boots are essential if any kind of

walking activity is planned. Break in the boots beforehand to prevent blisters, and keep a packet of plasters handy.

Pharmacies are called *Apótek* and are clearly named as such. They are open during business hours, with some continuing into the night. Most of Iceland's towns have at least one of them.

Iceland's medical facilities are excellent, but expensive. UK travellers are eligible for emergency medical treatment under EU reciprocal health schemes, as long as they are in possession of a European Health Insurance Card (EHIC). All travellers should take out comprehensive travel insurance before arrival.

It is very safe to walk along Iceland's streets even at night, particularly in Reykjavik at weekends, when the parties go on till the morning. However, it is always advisable to act sensibly, especially when the clubs close and drunken partygoers decide to head home. Even though it is very unusual, crime can happen, and it's best to be cautious and ensure your valuables are hidden. Policemen are around, although not highly visible. They appear at street events or occasions when crowds gather, but they remain fairly low-key, and are pretty much seen only when potentially needed.

OPENING HOURS

Banking hours are generally 09.15–16.00 Monday to Friday. At Keflavík Airport, Landsbanki is open on the first floor every day from 05.30–10.00 and 14.00–17.00, and in the departures hall from 05.30–18.00. Post offices are usually open 09.00–18.00 Monday to Friday and are closed at weekends.

Shopping hours are normally 09.00–18.00 Monday to Friday, and on Saturdays from 10.00 until anything between 13.00 and 16.00,

◀ *With a low crime rate, police in Reykjavik keep a low profile*

TRAVEL INSURANCE

However you book your city break, it is important to take out adequate personal travel insurance for the trip. For peace of mind the policy should give cover for medical expenses, loss, theft, repatriation, personal liability and cancellation expenses. If you are hiring a vehicle you should also check that you are appropriately insured and make sure that you take relevant insurance documents and your driving licence with you.

depending on the store. Supermarkets are open seven days a week, sometimes until as late as 23.00, although most close earlier.

Due to the country's location at such a northerly latitude, the amount of daylight varies dramatically between winter and summer and standard opening times can often change depending on the time of year. Office hours are 09.00–17.00, although in summer these times are put forward an hour, from 08.00–16.00.

Hours vary from museum to museum; some are closed on Monday and others do not even open outside the summer. It's best to check the individual places beforehand.

TOILETS

There are public toilets throughout central Reykjavik, and they are clearly marked WC. Some appear in the new Euro-style, looking like large circular advertising displays. They are free to use.

All restaurants and most coffee shops have public toilets. The locals don't mind outsiders visiting, although sometimes the number of cubicles are few, and the wait considerable. Discretion is advised!

Both the international and domestic airports are well supplied with public facilities.

CHILDREN

Children are very visible in Reykjavik, with parents taking them along whenever they can. It's not unusual to see a children's play area in cafés and restaurants, which keeps them entertained and out of harm's way while their parents relax over coffee or a meal. Festivals usually put on special events for children, and even the marathon has a 3 km event for young runners. You can download a free, comprehensive brochure on activities for families from ⓦ www.visitreykjavik.is (click 'Brochures & Map').

Lots of activities that are entertaining for adults are also fun for smaller folk, while others were set up with families in mind. If your kids are water babies you can take them along with you to one of Reykjavik's many heated swimming pools or thermal baths. Laugardalslaug (see page 102), with its waterslides and beach balls, is especially fun for young children.

Always popular with children is the Reykjavik Family Park & Zoo (see page 90). The Zoo specialises in Icelandic animals such as foxes and reindeer and kids can even ride an Icelandic horse, while the Family Park has theme park-style rides and activities. On the same site you'll find Science World, which older children enjoy for its hands-on activities and light-hearted focus on science and new technologies. Another fun museum is the Árbæjarsafn (see page 95), an outdoor museum village which succeeds in bringing the past alive. In summer there is also a petting zoo, where children can get to know chickens, goats, sheep and Icelandic horses.

If your kids just want some good old simple fun feeding the ducks, head straight to Tjörnin (see page 75), the huge City Pond right in the heart of town, which has an almost endless supply of ducks, geese, swans and migratory birds passing through on their way to sunnier climes.

The City Pond is popular with both ducks and children

COMMUNICATION

Internet

With computer usage one of the highest, per capita, in the world, the internet is a way of life in Iceland. Most information is given alternatively as a website and it's possible to find out just about anything online. There are several internet cafés in town and most coffee houses, bars and hotels have free wireless.

The Tourist Information Centre (see page 153) is a convenient location to check your email, and the purchase of the Reykjavik Welcome Card entitles the owner to free web usage here.

Phone

Iceland's public phones are few and far between, but when you do find one you can use coins, credit cards or pre-paid cards with them. Pre-paid cards can be purchased at post offices and service stations. Most people use mobile telephones, and foreign GSM systems work

TELEPHONING ICELAND

To call Iceland from abroad, dial your country's international access code (oo from the UK, o11 from the USA), then Iceland's country code (354), then the seven-digit number you require.

TELEPHONING ABROAD

To make an international call from Iceland, dial oo, then the relevant country code, followed by the area or city code (usually dropping the first 'o' if there is one) and then the local number. Some useful country codes are: UK 44, USA & Canada 1, Australia 61, New Zealand 64, Republic of Ireland 353, South Africa 72.

within the country. Mobile phones may be rented from Síminn, previously known as Iceland Telecom.

Iceland's country code is 354, followed by a seven-digit number. There are no area codes. Note that the Icelandic telephone directory lists entrants alphabetically by their first name rather than their surname.

Post

There are post offices in many of Iceland's towns, and several within Reykjavik. Stamps are also available at most places where postcards are sold. Post boxes are red, marked 'Pósturinn' in yellow letters.

Being halfway between Europe and North America, mail goes quickly between the continents, with, for example, a letter to the UK taking about three days to arrive. For further information, check out Ⓦ www.postur.is

ELECTRICITY

Electricity here works on the same system as the rest of Western Europe, with 220 volts (AC) and 50 hertz. The standard two-pin round-ended adapters are required for UK and US electrical items.

TRAVELLERS WITH DISABILITIES

Although not totally equipped for the visitors with disabilities, Iceland is reasonably good at providing facilities, especially with prior notice. Many hotels and some of the larger department stores are wheelchair accessible, although most places recommend travelling with an able-bodied companion. All international flights and coastal ferries are able to accommodate passengers with disabilities.

For advice on travelling in Iceland with a disability, try contacting **Sjálfsbjörg** (ⓐ Hátún 12, 105 Reykjavik ⓣ 550 0360 Ⓦ www.sjalfsbjorg.is ⓛ 09.15–16.15 Mon–Fri).

TOURIST INFORMATION

Tourist Information Centre ⓐ Aðalstræti 2, 101 ① 590 1500
Ⓦ www.visitreykjavik.is

Keflavík Airport Tourist Information Centre ⓐ Keflavík Airport,
235 Keflavík ① 425 6000 Ⓦ www.keflavikairport.com

Hafnarfjörður Tourist Office ⓐ Strandgata 6, Hafnarfjörður
① 585 5500 Ⓦ www.hafnarfjordur.is

North Iceland Tourist Information Centre ⓐ Hafnarstræti 82, 600
Akureyri ① 462 3300 Ⓦ www.nordurland.is

West Iceland Tourist Information Centre ⓐ Brúartorg, 310 Borgarnes
① 437 2214 Ⓦ www.west.is

BACKGROUND READING

The Icelandic Sagas, e.g. *Njals Saga*
Dip into the Norse medieval world, and gain some understanding of
an integral part of Icelandic culture, by reading these 12–14th-century
stories that are part history, part adventure.

The Works of Halldór Laxness
Writing in his own language, the home-grown Nobel Laureate wrote
several books based on Icelanders themselves and is considered one
of the greatest European novelists of the 20th century. His works are
available in translated editions.

Emergencies

In any emergency, contact the police, ambulance or fire service on ☏ 112

MEDICAL EMERGENCIES

For an emergency 24-hour doctor in the Reykjavik area, call ☏ 1770. Alternatively, go to the Emergency department (*Slysadeild*) at the **National University Hospital** (🅐 Fossvogur ☏ 543 2000).

Doctors and dentists are listed in the phone book. Alternatively, ask at your hotel or local tourist office. Virtually all medical practitioners in the country speak English.

Emergency dentists can be found by calling ☏ 575 0505 or checking 🅦 www.tannsi.is.

Emergency pharmacies (*Apótek*)

There are two pharmacies in Reykjavik that are open longer hours than usual:

Lyf og heilsa 🅐 Háaleitisbraut 68 ☏ 581 2101 🕐 09.00–22.00

Lyfja 🅐 Lágmúli 5 ☏ 533 2300 🕐 07.00–01.00

POLICE

If you require police assistance in an emergency, dial ☏ 112 from any phone or mobile phone. For other enquiries, including lost property, the police station is located in the centre of Reykjavik at 🅐 Hverfisgata 113, 101 ☏ 444 1000 🕐 08.00–16.00 Mon–Fri

EMBASSIES & CONSULATES

All embassies are located in Reykjavik unless otherwise stated.

EMERGENCY PHRASES

Help! Hjálp! *Hyowlp!*

Call an ambulance/a doctor/the police!
Náið í sjúkrabíl/lækni/lögregluna!
Now-ith ee syookrahbeel/layekni/lerg-rehglunah!

Can you help me?
Getur þú hjálpað mér?
Gehter thoo hyowlpahth myehr?

Australia Embassy ⓐ Dampfaergevej 26, 2100 Copenhagen, Denmark ⓣ +45 7026 3676 ⓦ www.denmark.embassy.gov.au ⓒ 08.30–16.30 Mon–Thur, 08.30 16.00 Fri

Canada Embassy ⓐ Túngata 14, 101 ⓣ 575 6500 ⓦ www.canada.is ⓒ 00.90–12.00 or by appointment

Republic of Ireland Embassy ⓐ Østbanegade 21, 2100 Copenhagen, Denmark ⓣ +45 3542 3233 ⓦ www.embassyofireland.dk ⓒ 10.00–12.30, 14.30–16.30 Mon–Fri

South Africa Embassy ⓐ Drammensveien 88C, 0204 Oslo, Norway ⓣ +47 2327 3220 ⓦ www.saemboslo.no ⓒ 08.00–16.00 Mon–Fri

UK Embassy ⓐ Laufásvegur 31, 101 ⓣ 550 5100 ⓦ www.ukiniceland.fco.gov.uk ⓒ 08.30–16.00 Mon–Thur, 08.30–15.30 Fri

USA Embassy ⓐ Laufásvegur 21, 101 ⓣ 562 9100 ⓒ http://iceland.usembassy.gov ⓒ 08.00–17.00 Mon–Fri

Editorial/project management: Lisa Plumridge
Copy editor: Monica Guy
Layout/DTP: Alison Rayner

The publishers would like to thank the following individuals and organisations for supplying the copyright photographs for this book: big-ashb, page 107; Christopher Bolwig, page 12; James Cridland, pages 35 & 57; Jared Goralnick, page 55; Jon Helgason/iStockphoto.com, page 31; Pat Hinsley, page 48; Stephan Hoerold/iStockphoto.com, page 23; M Wolfe/SXC.hu, page 141; Ethel Davies, all others.

Send your thoughts to
books@thomascook.com

- **Found a great bar, club, shop or must-see sight that we don't feature?**
- **Like to tip us off about any information that needs a little updating?**
- **Want to tell us what you love about this handy little guidebook and more importantly how we can make it even handier?**

Then here's your chance to tell all! Send us ideas, discoveries and recommendations today and then look out for your valuable input in the next edition of this title.

Email the above address (stating the title) or write to:
pocket guides Series Editor, Thomas Cook Publishing, PO Box 227, Coningsby Road, Peterborough PE3 8SB, UK.

WHAT'S IN YOUR GUIDEBOOK?

Independent authors Impartial up-to-date information from our travel experts who meticulously source local knowledge.

Experience Thomas Cook's 165 years in the travel industry and guidebook publishing enriches every word with expertise you can trust.

Travel know-how Thomas Cook has thousands of staff working around the globe, all living and breathing travel.

Editors Travel-publishing professionals, pulling everything together to craft a perfect blend of words, pictures, maps and design.

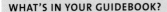

You, the traveller We deliver a practical, no-nonsense approach to information, geared to how you really use it.

Useful phrases

English	Icelandic	Approx pronunciation
BASICS		
Yes	Já	*Yow*
No	Nei	*Nay*
Please	Takk	*Tak*
Thank you	Takk fyrir	*Tak feerir*
Hello	Halló	*Hahlo*
Goodbye	Bless	*Bless*
Excuse me	Afsakið	*Åfsahkith*
Sorry	Mér þykir það leitt	*Myehr thikir thath leyht*
That's okay	Allt í lagi	*Ahlt ee layi*
I don't speak Icelandic	Ég tala ekki íslensku	*Yehkh tala ekki ees-len-skoo*
Do you speak English?	Talar þú ensku?	*Talahr thoo ensku?*
Good morning	Góðan daginn	*Gohthahn dayin*
Good afternoon	Góðan daginn	*Gohthahn dayin*
Good evening	Gott kvöld	*Gott kvult*
Goodnight	Góða nótt	*Goh-thah noht*
My name is ...	Ég heiti ...	*Yehkh heyti ...*
NUMBERS		
One	Einn	*Aydn*
Two	Tveir	*Tvehr*
Three	Þrír	*Threer*
Four	Fjórir	*Fyohrrir*
Five	Fimm	*Fim*
Six	Sex	*Sex*
Seven	Sjö	*Syuh*
Eight	Átta	*Owtah*
Nine	Níu	*Nee-er*
Ten	Tíu	*Tee-er*
Twenty	Tuttugu	*Terterkher*
Fifty	Fimmtíu	*Fimtee-er*
One hundred	Eitt hundrað	*Eht hundrahth*
SIGNS & NOTICES		
Airport	Flugvöllur	*Flergvutlur*
Smoking	Reykingar	*Raykingar*
No smoking	Reyklaus	*Rayklios*
Toilets	Snyrting	*Snirting*
Ladies/Gentlemen	Konur/Karlar	*Kohnur/Katlar*
Open/Closed	Opið/Lokað	*Ohpith/Lohkath*
Bus	Strætó	*Strigh-toe*